Government Policy and Critical Success Factors of Small Businesses in Singapore

Government Policy and Critical Success Factors of Small Businesses in Singapore

By

Harold Siow Song Teng

CAMBRIDGE
SCHOLARS
PUBLISHING

Government Policy and Critical Success Factors of Small Businesses in Singapore,
by Harold Siow Song Teng

This book first published 2011

Cambridge Scholars Publishing

12 Back Chapman Street, Newcastle upon Tyne, NE6 2XX, UK

British Library Cataloguing in Publication Data
A catalogue record for this book is available from the British Library

ISBN (10): 1-4438-3352-5, ISBN (13): 978-1-4438-3352-3

Dedicated to my loving wife, the one and only Vicky TTL

TABLE OF CONTENTS

LIST OF TABLES

PREFACE

The difficulties of implementing relevant policies that can successfully transform a nation's economy from a poor developing backwater into a highly industrialized economy are legendary. One of the essential sectors responsible for propelling a country's economy forward is that of the small businesses. From politics to economic policies, the State determines the way how businesses (including small businesses) are being run. The right combination of good government policies for business and a spirit of entrepreneurship among current and aspiring business owners can help develop a healthy entrepreneurial climate, which forms the basis for economic growth.

This book examines in detail, the various types of initiatives undertaken by the Singaporean government to assist businesses and promote entrepreneurship and would appeal to readers from the business community in general and small businesses in particular, along with government officials, business academics, students and the general public. The book also looks at the policies being taken, during the global financial crisis years (2008-2009) to assist businesses and their effectiveness. In addition, the book utilizes a simple business model which allows businesses to use as a checklist, to examine where their firms stand, and also as a personal leadership ability self-appraisal.

The business leaders could better understand how to pursue their ultimate goal of ensuring business successes with better personnel management and leadership training by for example, taking more business management and leadership courses and personal development. Government business policy makers could ensure that they continue to implement high quality, pro-business policies that support the business community in general and small businesses in particular, with relevant industry consultation and at the same time, working together with the employer associations and unions to achieve mutually agreeable industry and business outcomes.

Public policy makers and others could utilize such a model to assess a firm's potential for success so that society could benefit in direct and indirect ways via the allocation of limited resources (government aid, loans and so forth) toward higher-potential firms. In a globally competitive business environment in which a high premium is placed both upon entrepreneurship and management effectiveness, the theoretical elaboration and practical application of such knowledge will be beneficial.

ACKNOWLEDGEMENTS

I am most grateful to God for her love, care and guidance throughout all the ups and downs I have experienced in my life, including the difficulties I have gone through while pursuing my PhD, upon which this book is based. I would like to also thank my supervisor Professor Sajid Anwar for his guidance and supervision, without which my PhD would not have been accomplished.

I am deeply indebted to my family, especially my wife Vicky, whose love, support and constant encouragement made this book possible. I would also like to offer my sincere thanks to my program director Dr Marguerite Kolar in Australia, my good friend Dr Gurpreet Singh Bhatia for his guidance on econometrics.

I would like to thank my employer and colleagues at the East Asian Institute (EAI), National University of Singapore. It was while working as a researcher for the EAI from 2006 to 2009 which had provided me with the intellectual motivation and drive, to challenge myself academically, which led me to enroll in the PhD program at the International Graduate School of Business (IGSB), University of South Australia in 2007.

Last but not least, I would also like to thank my former employers, the Singapore Ministry of Information, Communications & the Arts (MICA), as well as International Enterprise Singapore (IE Singapore), with whom I had the privilege of serving from 2009-2010, before rejoining academia once again in late 2010.

ABSTRACT

This book proposes benchmarks that can be used by policy makers to improve the performance of SMEs in Singapore. Business leaders could pursue their goal of ensuring business successes with better personnel management and leadership training by for example, taking more business management and leadership courses and personal development. Government policy makers and others could utilize such a model to assess a firm's potential for success so that society could benefit via the allocation of limited resources toward higher-potential firms. The book introduces an exploratory business success versus failure prediction model, modeled after the Lussier (1995) prediction model, using data from Singapore. Using logistic regression analysis, it is found that the Lussier Model ($p = 0.057$) and the Exploratory Model ($p = 0.047$) are significant predictors of business success and failure.

The logistic regression and factor reduction methods are used to model the relationship between the success and failure of SMEs. Business success is being defined as an SME having made a profit in the past three years. It is found that Model 1 also known as the Exploratory Model is the most suitable predictor model. Using logistic regression modeling, this book finds that: 1) having good quality staff; 2) having good products that are either very new or established older products/ services; 3) having good customer relationships; 4) having good top leadership are the top four most important CSFs associated with business success. Using factor reduction onto Model 1, this book finds that: 1) having relevant past industry experience; 2) having a business plan; 3) having broad access to resources; 4) having good government policy; 5) having good business record keeping; and 6) having good customer relations are important CSFs for small businesses. The results from the two methodologies and interviews with the government business promotion agencies show that a list of CSFs does exist in the minds of small businesses and the variable 'good government policy' is an important CSF.

This book is original whereby the Exploratory Model accurately predicted 86.3 percent of the successful (or failed) firms. Using this model, researchers and interested parties could focus on an identifiable list of factors, to study the business performance of SMEs, as well as understand if government policy in general, has been beneficial to SME growth and development.

The data analysis presented in this book supports the hypotheses that (i) good government policy is an important CSF towards the success of SMEs, (ii) successful SMEs tend to have a list of CSFs which they can identify and adhere to, and (iii) it is possible to forecast the potential success/failure of a firm using a prediction model. It is surprising that while pursuing their respective business activities, the SMEs surveyed in this study regarded government policy and the availability of business finance though important, amongst other factors, of lesser importance compared to the above-mentioned nine broad variables (good customer relationship appeared twice).

It is recommended that policy makers and others could use the model to assess a firm's potential for success and society can benefit in direct or indirect ways via the reallocation of limited resources be it government aid, loans etc, towards higher-potential firms.

CHAPTER ONE

INTRODUCTION

1.1 Background

In the immediate aftermath of World War II, Singapore was still a British colony struggling to develop economically. Singapore achieved self-government in 1959 and full independence only in 1965. Economic growth in Singapore started to take a foothold only in the 1960s, spurred on by increases in foreign direct investments (FDI) and domestic savings. In the 1960s gross national product (GNP) per capita was less than US$320 (EDB 2010).

Since gaining independence, Singapore has successfully transformed its economy from a small regional entrepot into a highly international and industrialized economy. From 1965 till the 1997 Asian financial crisis, the Singaporean economy grew at an annual average rate of over 8.5% (Hew 2004). In spite of its constraints such as its small land size (just about 700 square kilometers) and lack of natural resources, Singapore has become one of the world's most open and competitive economies. Today with a per capita GNP of US$34,760, Singapore has one of the highest per capita incomes in the world (World Bank 2010).

One of the main economic players responsible for Singapore's economic success is its small and medium-sized enterprises or SMEs. Their overall success has helped propel the country and its people forward. From economic policies to politics, Singapore is a planned and regulated economy. Singapore's economic success story is actually the result of a form of capitalism carefully calibrated and controlled by the government. The Singapore government's interventions and initiations have largely been successful as far as the Singapore economy is concerned. This is an anomaly which many other countries have been unable to replicate successfully.

The policies underlying Singapore's economic success are partially illustrated in the way many businesses (including small businesses) are being run. Singapore displays many of the features associated with a healthy entrepreneurial and pro-business climate, spurred on by deliberate government policy. This book aims to examine and understand the main factors that make small businesses successful in Singapore. This study uses a non-theoretical approach to explore variables (on critical success factors) from past literature, to find the underlying factors small businesses in Singapore believe to be critical to their success.

1.2 Necessity, Value & Aim of Research

Why are SMEs so important to Singapore? Despite the limitations associated with their size, SMEs produce not only more jobs, but also more innovations than large companies. Empirical research has revealed that small firms in the United States spend almost twice as much of their research and development (R & D) dollars in fundamental research as do large firms. This finding provides an alternative to the conventional perception of SMEs being dependent on large firms. Being small enables SMEs to be potentially more flexible and nimble in making changes and exploiting new opportunities compared to larger firms (Yeung & Chew 2001).

Singapore has a large and vibrant community of some 148,000 SMEs in 2007. Together they make up 99 percent of all enterprises, employ six out of every 10 workers and account for 48 percent of total value added in the economy making this group of business enterprises worthwhile studying (Spring Singapore 2008). A recent 2010 publication of the Singapore government suggests that the figures remain largely unchanged with SMEs still accounting for 99 percent of all enterprises, 62 percent of the workforce and 50 percent of GDP. SMEs in the Association of South East Asian Nations (ASEAN) too, account for 99 percent of all enterprises, 70 percent of the workforce and 40 percent of GDP (IE Singapore Work Plan 2010).

According to Singapore SME 2010, SMEs are generally defined as having the following: 1) at least 30 percent local equity (owned by Singapore residents); 2) fixed productive assets (defined as net book value of factory building, machinery and equipment) not exceeding S$15 million (US$11.1 million); 3) employment size not exceeding 200 workers for non-manufacturing companies in the Singaporean context. This is consistent with the European (European Network for SME Research 1995) and American (United States Government Printing Office 1995) definitions of SMEs.

The rationale or formative thinking behind this book project stems from the fact that many countries, particularly developing ones, want to encourage the growth of SMEs for economic development. Singapore has prospered under deliberate government industrial and specific SME Policies and could serve as an example for these countries.

This book aims to do three things, namely: 1) provide an in-depth critical evaluation of the evolution of government policy in Singapore towards SMEs; 2) identify critical success factors (CSFs) of SMEs; and 3) develop a success/failure prediction model. The aims of this book could be summarized into the following three hypotheses:

H1: ***Good government policy is an important CSF towards the success of SMEs;***
H2: ***Successful SMEs have a list of CSFs which they can identify & adhere to;***
H3: ***It is possible to forecast the potential success or failure of a firm using a prediction model.***

Singapore has prospered under deliberate government industrial and specific SME policies. 'Research on the prediction of success and failure of businesses can potentially benefit many: would-be and current small business owners; those who assist, train and advise them; those who provide capital for their ventures; their suppliers; and public policy makers' (Lussier & Pfeifer 2001, p. 229).

It is worth noting that government support for SMEs is increasing in wealthy countries. This is based on the view that SMEs contribute to high-quality employment generation and are exceptionally innovative, as well as the perception that SMEs are more flexible and responsive to the demands of consumers (Parker 2000).

According to Feindt et al (2002), 'most firms do not grow; only very rapidly growing companies call Gazelles do' and that consists of only about 3 percent of all small companies in the European Union (EU). The EU has 16 million companies, of which 99 percent employ fewer than 250 people; 93 percent are micro-enterprises with fewer than 10 employees

(Feindt et al 2002, p. 51). This shows the importance and the need to study SMEs and the reasons for their success or failure in greater detail.

In order for SMEs to operate effectively in the marketplace, two main types of conditions must be in place. First of all, appropriate government policy conducive for small businesses ought to be present. Secondly, SMEs that are successful usually have a list of factors which they have followed closely and adhered to, which allowed them to achieve business success. All SMEs must have a list of things or factors that they have 'to get it right' in order for their particular businesses in question to be successful. As such, an SME's success or failure could potentially be predicted from such a list of success/ failure factors.

1.3 Book Outline

The first chapter of this book begins by introducing the necessity and value of understanding and identifying the vital factors otherwise known as the critical success factors (CSFs) that enterprises ought to possess, so as to be able to maximize their opportunities of business success and reduce the chances of failure.

Chapter 2, the first of two literature review chapters, discusses the relevant literature on government policies over the years since Singapore's independence, from the initial years of experimenting with industrialization to Singapore's gradual economic success and prosperity till date. This chapter also looks at the relevant government policy on small businesses regarded as being important by international scholars studying CSFs in the business field.

Chapter 3, the second literature review chapter, discusses the relevant academic literature over recent years, from the initial evolution of the concept of CSFs to their gradual adoption and popular usage till date. The short listing of the various CSFs and the different models in this chapter is achieved through the literature review of academic research on the CSFs of businesses globally.

Chapter 4 outlines the research methodology of the book and explores the methods which have been used by other relevant researchers in the past and also at present. The details of questionnaire survey design, data collection etc are discussed in this chapter.

Chapter 5 provides an analysis of the empirical results and finalizes the results of the research. It also explains the meaning and implications of the research findings and interprets what each of the respective variable means in the context of this book.

This book concludes with Chapter 6 where the final research outcomes are being discussed, whereby the initial three research questions of this book are considered and linked to the results of the empirical study. Recommendations for future research are also touched on.

CHAPTER TWO

GOVERNMENT POLICY TOWARDS SMEs

2.1 Introduction

In Singapore the government plays a very active role in assisting businesses in general by providing a conducive environment for the growth and development of businesses and especially SMEs. 'The Singaporean government is strongly of the view that often all it takes is a great idea to create business success; the government is also of the belief that while many successful companies started as SMEs and succeeded by their own merits, others needed a little help since not everyone has the resources or expertise to take their ideas, products or services onto the world stage' says Ted Tan, Deputy CEO of IE Singapore (Tan 2009).[1] This chapter includes a review of related literature and an analysis of government policy toward SMEs. It discusses the main government initiatives from education policy to industrial policy and business policy, since Singapore's early years as a nation, to help SMEs achieve their full potential in Singapore and beyond. The respective academic literature that supports these initiatives is also discussed.

Anwar et al (2004), Kim & Lau (1994), Wade (1990), Krause (1987) all argue that government policies have resulted in massive FDI into Singapore and government expenditure on education and training has resulted in the increased availability of skilled labour. Besides FDI and government spending on education; government expenditure on research and development (R & D); trade and industry; lower taxation etc, have also greatly benefitted the Singaporean economy (Anwar 2004, p. 375). Other indirect actions of the government include the introduction of incentives in encouraging Singaporeans to save more resulting in a higher rate of national saving, which in turn means that there are more funds available for long term investments in the above mentioned areas of the Singaporean economy.

In addition, Anwar (2006) found that investments in human capital are vital for the growth of a country's economy, including its manufacturing industry. Anwar et al (2004) also examined the role of the government in Singapore's manufacturing industry and found that government policies in attracting FDI and government spending in education play very important roles in maximizing the country's industrial successes. The following sections discuss what Anwar (2006, 2004), Hew (2004), Kim and Lau (1994), Wade (1990), Krause (1987) and the rest have examined on the relevant government policies in greater detail and outline their implications and effectiveness on the state of development of SMEs in Singapore.

Table 1 below sums up the development stages of countries including that of Singapore. In the 1960s and 1970s, Singapore began as an original equipment manufacturing (OEM) economy whereby local firms learned the assembly process for standard simple goods from foreign MNCs. In the 1980s, local Singaporean firms learned process engineering and detailed product design skills from foreign MNCs and gained more value-add to the manufacturing process with their own design and manufacturing (ODM). From the 1990s till the present day, local Singaporean firms conduct manufacturing, product design, and R & D for new products and many have started to own their own brands and manufacturing (OBM) abilities.

Table 1: Stages of Latecomer Development

Period/ Stage	***Technological Transition***	***Market Transition***
1960s/ 1970s Original Equipment Manufacture (OEM)	Local firm learns assembly process for standard simple goods	Foreign MNC/ buyer designs, brands and distributes. Also gains non-manufacturing value added
1980s Own Design & Manufacture (ODM)	Local firm learns process engineering and detailed product design skills	As with above, MNC buys, brands and distributes. MNC gains manufacturing value added
1990s Own-Brand Manufacture (OBM)	Local firm conducts manufacturing, product design, and R & D for new products	Local firm has own brand, organizes distribution and captures all value added

NB: MNC – Multinational corporations; R & D – Research and Development
Source: Adapted from ADB (2003)

2.2 Human Capital Development

Since independence in 1965, Singapore's educational system has been through a series of reforms. The policies resulting from these educational reforms have made Singapore a very attractive place for foreign MNCs to come and setup subsidiary companies in Singapore because there is always a pool of relatively highly skilled labour available. The Goh Report (1979) saw the introduction of streaming as the means by which the demand for education would be managed, with schools providing general and academic education and vocational institutes providing vocational education for those students who did not progress well along the traditional academic route.

However, these initial attempts to incorporate vocational and technical education into the curriculum had to be revised because of the low status attached to vocational education. The government did not always get it right. Further reforms were therefore introduced in 1990 to increase the minimum period of education to ten years and upgrade technical education, establishing the Institute of Technical Education (ITE). Higher education has been expanded but access is strictly controlled with the state retaining a clear distinction between the technical and technological orientation of the polytechnics and the academic orientation of the universities (Ashton & Sung, 1997).

On the industrial front, Singapore took advantage of its position as an entrepot trade centre, building on its trading advantages in the oil and chemical industries; other types of industries such as precision engineering and semi-conductor manufacturing were also attracted to the island. In addition to these, the electronics and electrical industries were also attracted to establish themselves in Singapore, where the capital, managerial expertise and technological capabilities were provided by MNCs such as Japan's Hitachi and Germany's Siemens corporations. As of December 2007, Singapore had a small economy with a labour force of 2,730,800, comprising of 1,830,000 locals and 900,800 foreigners (Singapore Manpower Report 2008, p. 56); the range of industries it could support was limited. Thus, when the government sought to move the economy in the direction of higher value-added forms of goods and services, it made sense to build on the initial, fairly narrow manufacturing base and focus on electronics, precision engineering and chemicals. In the services sector, the government pushed for the development of banking, financial and business services, where Singapore already has a competitive advantage in the region (Huff 1995); Singapore's early years as a former British colonial trading outpost gave it a natural advantage in the services industry.

Table 2: Technological Stages in Southeast Asia's Electronic Industry

Decade	*Singapore*	*Malaysia*	*Thailand*	*Indonesia*	*Vietnam*
1960s	Assembly	-	-	-	-
1970s	Process Engineering	Assembly	Assembly	-	-
1980s	Product Development	Process Engineering	Assembly	Assembly	Assembly
1990s	Research & Industry	Product Development	Process Engineering	Process Engineering	Assembly

Source: ADB (2003)

Before the 1980s, there were no specific SME policies in place in Singapore. Most SME related policies were introduced only after the 1980s. The priority was to attract FDI into Singapore, to develop the local industries and therefore help solve the critical issue of unemployment. Many policies were formulated to help SMEs and create a conducive environment for them to function. One of the most direct ways to help foreign SMEs establish in Singapore is to attract foreign business missions to visit Singapore and by marketing Singapore as a country with a strong support network of industries. By successfully attracting foreign investments into Singapore, the government is able to generate employment and at the same time, help local industries gain the technical and capital know-how for industrialization as well as encourage population growth (Ngiam 2011).

For example in 1999, Singapore's total active labour force (Citizens, Non-Citizen Residents and Work permit/ Employment pass holders) was 2.2 million and by 2006, the labour force had grown to 2.6 million (Yearbook of Statistics Singapore 2010). This is a growth of about 18 percent whereas the corresponding average annual population growth rate of Singaporean citizens from 1990 till 2006 was only 1.1 percent. The stock of FDI during the same time period grew from S$170 billion (US$126 billion) to over S$310 billion (US$229 billion) (Yearbook of Statistics Singapore 2010). One could argue that the rapid increase in FDI provided the conditions for such a sharp rise in employment opportunities. The rise in FDI itself partially contributed to the creation of entire systems of SMEs supporting foreign MNCs, and with the other local SMEs growing alongside, this created an impetus for the collective growth of the SME community in Singapore.[2] This is in line with the research by Anwar (2006 & 2004) where he argues that the Singaporean government's pro-business and pro-FDI policies have helped Singapore and its people prosper.

2.2.1 Problems Faced in Establishing the SME Sector

During independent Singapore's early years, one of the main problems faced by the government centered on training enough skilled labour to support the MNCs. This problem still exists today, but on a smaller scale. First, the Singapore government had to push the MNCs into producing higher value-added forms of production such as high-end semi-conductor manufacturing and the manufacturing of advance pharmaceutical products. Second, with only a small labour force, one of the main problems Singapore faced was how to ensure that all groups within the labour force were provided with the appropriate skills, especially as many of the older workers were educated only up to the primary level. The third challenge involved ensuring the transfer of technological capabilities (brought in by the MNCs) to the indigenous Singaporean population.

The first problem of encouraging high value added production by the MNCs was tackled through the introduction of the Skills Development Fund; a tax levied on low paid labour which thereby discourages employers from using cheap labour. The Fund is used to 'up-skill' the workforce i.e. to provide the financial resources to train the workers. However, the MNCs are reluctant to fund the up-skilling of older workers initially, as their representatives see the lack of secondary education as the responsibility of the government. The up-skilling of older workers is tackled through a variety of programs delivered through employers but funded through the Skills Development Board. These include the Basic Education for Skills Training program (1983), and the Modular Skills Training program (1986), for those in manufacturing, and the Core Skills for Effectiveness and Change (1987) for those in the service sector. In this way the government sought to upgrade the skills of the most vulnerable workers and keep them attractive to employers. In this task they had some success. For example, by 1992, 78% of the target group of 225,000 workers had experienced at least one module of the Basic Education for Skill Training program (ITE 1993). Till the present day, the Skills Development Fund continues to exist.

The government has also used a similar approach to upgrade the skills of workers who are already employed in leading edge companies to prepare them for the next wave of challenges. Working with major companies, the government introduced programs aimed at deepening workers' skills through structured on-the-job (OJT) training. These OTJ blueprints, modeled on the Japanese system of OTJ, have been developed with major employers in each of the industries targeted for growth and then cascaded down through other employers in the same industry. Since being introduced in 1993, over 100,000 workers had been through the scheme by 1997(Ashton & Sung, 1997). Similar techniques are still being used to improve workers' problem solving abilities. Using these and other programs, the government has sought to supplement the training provided by MNCs to ensure that the national skill needs, as opposed to the company's skills needs, are met.

The other way in which the government has sought to enhance workers' skills is through the introduction of schemes designed to support the establishment of occupational labour markets. Employers in engineering and related industries require workers trained in intermediate level skills but would not voluntarily underwrite the costs of training. The government therefore established the New Apprenticeship Scheme in 1990 modeled on the German dual system, but modeled to suit local conditions. More highly specialized skills were embedded in the workforce through Joint Industrial Training Centers, developed in collaboration with major MNCs (e.g. Shell Eastern Petroleum Ltd and Texas Instrument) since the 1970s. The Centers provided high level training in electronics and precision engineering.

As the demand shifted toward more knowledge and technology-intensive industries, the scope of providing training was extended to incorporate knowledge from other MNCs and foreign governments (Wong 1993). Another distinctive feature of the Singaporean system is the incorporation of labour into the skill formation process. Following the successful suppression of the communists in the then British Malaya (Singapore and Malaysia today) by the 1960s, the Singapore government successfully incorporated the numerous trade unions that existed at that time into the machinery of a government-directed central umbrella of trade unions, the National Trades Union Congress (NTUC). Today, the NTUC still plays a significant role in both delivering skills training and encouraging employers to up-skill their labour forces (Goh & Green 1997).

The use of the MNCs to provide the capital, technology and managerial expertise, together with the existence of a small labour force, had important implications for the subsequent development of the educational and training system. First of all, the system has to deliver progressively higher level skills across a relatively narrow range of industries. This meant that it had to be focused in terms of the types of skills developed in the secondary and higher education system. Second, the use of MNCs to provide capital and technological know-how meant that ways had to be found to ensure that the new skills acquired were firmly embedded in the local labour force. Third, given the concern of MNCs with their own immediate training needs, there was always a danger that the long term skill needs of the economy would be overlooked. MNCs could not be relied upon to move in the direction of forms of higher value-added production on their own account. Fourth, the small size of the labour force meant maximum use had to be made of all groups of workers (Aston et al 2002, p. 17). These are the distinctive conditions which subsequently helped shape the Singaporean educational and training system till it is today.

In the transformation from a developing to a newly industrialized economy, Singapore initiated the first SME Master Plan in 1989. The SME Master Plan is a comprehensive, detailed list of actions to systematically facilitate the growth of the SME sector in Singapore while focusing broadly on promoting domestic entrepreneurship and innovation; increasing informational market efficiency by encouraging information exchange and improving the dissemination of information about new methods and opportunities; promoting best practices in business through easy access to consultancy adoption and training; and encouraging domestic enterprises to grow and expand internationally (SME Committee, 1989). This marked the true beginning of Singapore's journey to systematically develop local SMEs.

Singapore then gradually upgraded its local expertise so that the country could sustain its international competitiveness, so as to attract more MNCs to relocate to the island. This differentiates Singapore from other countries in the region. A follow-up plan called the SME 21 Plan was released in 2000 to ensure the relevance of the existing available programs to help make SMEs more resilient and to be innovative in the increasingly competitive environment especially in the region. The SME 21 Plan adopts a three-pronged strategic approach to SME development, namely: 1) enterprise-level SME development; 2) sector-level SME development; and 3) broad-based SME development strategies (see Appendix C for more details).[3] The SME 21 Plan is a comprehensive plan to develop strong linkages between MNCs and SMEs, so that both groups complement each other and serve the export-oriented industry along with providing employment to the Singapore economy. These policies and initiatives are in line with the findings of scholars such as Hew (2004) in that the SME policies of the Singapore government do indeed help create a conducive atmosphere for business and enterprise to flourish in Singapore, especially for SMEs.

2.2.2 Industrialization Policy

Early industrialization policy in Singapore is tasked to the Ministry of Trade and Industry (MTI), whose agenda dominated that of other ministries. MTI still shapes most of Singapore's industrial policy today, though there are increasingly more inputs from all other spectrums of society including businesses, academia and other government agencies. Its representatives chair the various Boards and Councils which form the decision making process in those departments dealing with the provision of education and training. This ensures that the requirements of the government's industrial strategy take precedence over those of the vested interests of any one Ministry or Board.

The Economic Development Board (EDB) aids the MTI in its task of implementing the industrial strategies. It is the task of the EDB to ensure that inward investment is forthcoming to provide capital for the new industries. In performing this function, the EDB is also cognizant of the human resource requirements for those industries. The skill requirements of those industries together with those of existing employers then shape the national skill requirements. Other inputs into the formulation of national skill needs are derived from the national objectives concerning the type of industries the country wishes to attract (including industries in the near future). For example, the government recently sought to increase the number of companies operating in the field of research and development. For this to happen, an increase in the output of scientists and engineers is urgently required. This requirement is then fed into the industrial policy equation and the result is that there is a tremendous increase in the international recruitment of top scientists, engineers and other R & D professionals into Singapore. This is in addition to the sharp rise in the number of local scholarships being given out to Singaporean students to study in top universities abroad in the United States and Europe etc, and the local universities. This is in line with the research done by Anwar et al (2004), Kim and Lau (1994), Wade (1990) and Krause (1987) on the attracting of talented people to work for and work in Singapore.

All the above information on national skills needs are then collated by the Council for Professional and Technical Education (CPTE). On the supply side, the education and training institutions produce data on their existing and projected outputs. Academics provide an analysis of national data which, together with the other inputs are used to identify what the education and training system can deliver. On the basis of these analyses, judgments are then made about the future level of output from the education and training institutions and whether it will be necessary to fill any gaps by recruiting appropriately skilled labor from outside the country. This information is then used by the CPTE to establish specific targets for the various components of the education and training system, i.e., the Universities, Polytechnics, schools and the Institutes for Technical Education. On the training front, targets for on-the-job and work-based training and for employers' investment in training are set by the then Singapore Productivity and Standards Board (Spring Singapore today); today, it is the responsibility of the Workforce Development Agency (WDA) to ensure that the skills of the labor force are upgraded to meet the demands of existing and new industries and that the supply of labor is sufficient to meet existing and anticipated demand (Ashton & Sung, 1997).

When taken together, the work of the CPTE and WDA provide sophisticated mechanisms to ensure when and by how much, the country's desired future skill needs are to be met specifically. These targets are then used to determine the output from the education system, from the technical education system, and as far as possible, from employers' own training activities. These mechanisms function efficiently because both politicians and civil servants share the same objectives while the technocrats operate through a corporate culture which facilitates rapid decision making while minimizing bureaucratic procedures (Schein 1996).

2.3 Whole-of-Government (WOG) Outcome

One important central strategic outcome that has been identified by the Singapore government is something that has been termed the Whole-of-Government (WOG) Outcome. The central idea of WOG is that all actions taken by the government collectively (i.e. through the various ministries and Statutory Boards and agencies) must lead to the same strategic macro outcomes. There are currently six clusters of strategic outcomes that have been identified namely:

1. Sustainable Economic Growth
2. Robust Social Security System
3. World-class Living Environment and Infrastructure
4. Secure and Influential Singapore
5. Strong families and Cohesive Society
6. A High-Performance Government

These six clusters of strategic outcomes are collectively worked upon through Cluster Strategic Reviews with the various ministries, Statutory Boards and agencies.[4]

2.4 Finance

In just over four decades since independence, Singapore has established itself as a thriving financial centre of international repute, serving not only its domestic economy, but also the wider Asia Pacific region and the world. Singapore's financial centre offers a broad range of financial services including banking, insurance, investment banking and treasury services.

A key aspect of Singapore's financial centre is its deep and liquid capital markets. With one of the more well-established capital markets in Asia-Pacific, the Singapore Exchange (SGX) is the preferred listing location for more than 200 global companies. Today, Singapore has grown to be the largest Real Estate Investment Trust (REITs) market in Asia ex-Japan and also provides an extensive offering of investments in business trusts of shipping, aviation and infrastructure assets (MAS 2010).

Singapore's bond market has also grown significantly. With an extensive range of both Singapore government securities and foreign corporate bonds available, Singapore offers fixed income investors a wide range of investment opportunities. An established and well functioning capital market system as noted by Lawton (2002) is an important ingredient for business firms to raise funding for their business expansion and growth.

As one of the top 5 most active foreign exchange trading centers in the world, Singapore is also the second largest over-the-counter derivatives trading centre in Asia, and a leading commodities derivatives trading hub.

With total assets under management of around S$1 trillion (US$740 billion), and which continues to see steady growth, Singapore is also recognized as one of the premier asset management locations in Asia (MAS 2010).

Anwar (2006) notes that Singapore is one of the few regional economies that are not significantly affected by the Asian financial crisis. The Singaporean economy registered negative growth in 1998 but the growth rate was positive again in 1999 and 2000. The continued recession in Japan and a slowdown in the American economy contributed to negative gross domestic product (GDP) growth in 2001. Some studies have also indicated that although the Singaporean currency depreciated against the US dollar, it registered at least a 40 percent appreciation against its major ASEAN (Association of South East Asian Nations) trading partners (also see Montes & Giap, 1999). The reasons behind Singapore's success in withstanding the crisis include its relatively modern and well-developed financial system (Anwar 2006, p. 382).

All these factors make Singapore very business friendly as business loans; general funding, companies' stock exchange listing etc are all very easily available for firms to raise capital for their operations.

2.5 Conducive Business Environment

As an international financial centre, Singapore offers financial institutions a pro-business environment, excellent infrastructure, cost-competitiveness, a highly skilled and cosmopolitan labour force, and a strategic location in a region of opportunities.

Singapore has long been recognized as one of the best cities for business. In the Swiss-based international Institution for Management Development's 2008 World Competitiveness Yearbook, Singapore has been ranked as the second-most competitive country in the world after the United States. This is what a World Bank (2010) report says about doing business in Singapore: 'It takes an entrepreneur just over 6 working days to get a new business going in Singapore, with low start-up costs. Overall, taking into account other factors, including business licensing, taxes, credit legal rights and investor protection, Singapore have about the most business-friendly regulation in the world.'

Investors have also come to appreciate the high levels of transparency and reliability in business, economic and regulatory affairs in Singapore. A stable political structure with parliamentary democracy, a well-established judicial system, and the presence of strong domestic institutions with good corporate governance practices, have made the Singapore business environment even more attractive to global investors. Singapore has a robust and efficient legal and judicial framework and a well-regulated international financial sector. Singapore is the only Asian country with an "AAA" country rating (MAS 2010).

2.6 Excellent Infrastructure

Singapore's unique location and sophisticated telecommunications network allow financial institutions here to transact business with any part of the world within the same working day. International travel out of Singapore is equally convenient with more than 84 international airlines operating scheduled services through Singapore to more than 180 cities in 57 countries worldwide (MAS 2010).

2.7 Cost Competitiveness & the Existence of the Rule of Law

Singapore offers financial institutions a competitive tax rate environment. Singapore's corporate tax rate of 17 percent is one of the lowest in Asia-Pacific; only Hong Kong has a lower corporate rate of 16.5 percent. Singapore also offers the advantage of having a comprehensive network of Double Tax Agreements with more than 60 countries and continues to be cost competitive compared with other major cities (IRAS 2010). The existence of the rule of law and a clean and functioning judicial system also contributes to the competitiveness of the country as an international business hub.

2.8 Skilled Workforce & Attraction of Talent

Singapore boasts of a skilled workforce to meet industry demands. In addition to grooming the local workforce to meet the demand of the industry, Singapore also has an open door policy to international talent and expertise. Thousands of foreigners, from top investment bankers and scientists working in R & D to workers in the construction and domestic help industries are welcomed to Singapore through an efficient employment permit-based system. According to the latest available statistics, foreigners (non-Singaporeans residing in Singapore) comprise of one-third of the total population of 5.08 million i.e. over 1.6 million people (Singstat 2010). Washington-based risk consultancy agency, Business Environment Risk Intelligence (BERI), has rated Singapore's workforce as the world's best workers since 1980 (BERI 2010). According to the IMD World Competitiveness Yearbook 2010, Singapore has the most skilful and motivated labour force in the world (IMD 2010).

2.9 Strategic Location in a Region of Opportunities

Singapore is strategically located in a region of opportunities. Located at the heart of Southeast Asia, Singapore is well placed to serve the fast-growing markets of the Asia-Pacific region. Financial institutions in Singapore also trade around-the-clock with Asia-Pacific centers, as well as European and American centers, making Singapore a significant hub for 24-hour trading in foreign exchange and securities. International travel is equally convenient. Singapore has grown to be a strategic link and important gateway for global investors. This reinforces Lawton's (2002) study that a well and established capital market system is vital for SME and businesses in general, to raise funds for their businesses to grow.

Singapore seeks to ensure its relevance and connectivity to growth markets, not just in Asia but also beyond. As part of this initiative, Singapore has concluded Free Trade Agreements (FTAs) with major economies, including the United States, Japan, Korea, Australia, New Zealand, India and Jordon. There are ongoing FTA talks with other countries. These FTAs provide privileged access to the markets of partner countries. Beyond the immediate region, Singapore is also building linkages with countries further a-field including the Middle East, capitalizing on the growing trade and investment interests between these two regions (MAS 2010).

2.10 Key Government Agencies Set-up to Assist Businesses

In order to help business and enterprise grow and flourish in Singapore, the Singaporean government established several key government statutory boards aimed with the primary purposes of attracting FDI into Singapore; assisting and facilitating the ease of setting up small businesses in Singapore; and helping SMEs grow outwards from Singapore into the region and throughout the whole world. The following sub-sections explain what the Singaporean government has achieved in this area.

2.10.1 Economic Development Board (EDB) Singapore

The Economic Development Board of Singapore, the oldest government statutory body set-up in Singapore in the early 1960s to attract foreign direct investments (FDI) into Singapore, is the very first Singapore government organization tasked to promote economic development in Singapore.

EDB today is still tasked with attracting FDI, but is no longer tasked with helping SMEs in Singapore; the SME portfolio has been transferred to IE Singapore & Spring Singapore. These are one-stop agencies which facilitate and support local and foreign investors in both the manufacturing and services sectors, as they move up the value chain to achieve higher sustainable returns and seek out new business opportunities with a focus on expanding and extending existing industry verticals (EDB 2010).

2.10.2 International Enterprise (IE) Singapore

In 1983, the Singapore Trade Development Board (TDB) was first set up to assist Singaporean based businesses to expand out of Singapore, regionally and internationally. In 2002, the TDB was renamed and revamped as International Enterprise Singapore (IE Singapore). [5] IE Singapore's main focus industries span across eight key clusters including business services; electronics & precision engineering; information & communications technology; infrastructure services; environmental services; international trading; lifestyle; and transport & logistics services (IE Singapore 2010).

2.10.3 Spring Singapore

Spring Singapore is the enterprise development agency set up to help innovative companies grow and fostering a competitive SME sector. They work with partners to help enterprises in financing, capabilities and management development, technology and innovation, and access to markets. As the national standards and accreditation body, Spring Singapore also develops and promotes internationally-recognized standards and quality assurance to enhance competitiveness and facilitate trade.

The predecessor of Spring Singapore was the Singapore Productivity and Standards Board (PSB); the PSB itself was formed from the merger of the National Productivity Board (NPB) and the Singapore Institute of

Standards and Industrial Research (SISIR) in April 1996 (Spring Singapore 2010).[6]

In summary, the EDB helps attract FDI into Singapore which is beneficial for the country's employment, economic and technological growth. Spring Singapore helps and encourages the setting up and growth of businesses, especially SMEs, within Singapore. IE Singapore assists businesses including SMEs expand beyond Singapore into the world. There are some areas of overlapping, complementarities and competitiveness among these three agencies as all three target the growth of business enterprises in Singapore. However, such overlapping ensures that little or no SMEs fall through the cracks within the system which is certainly of benefit to SMEs.

2.11 Key Government Assistance Programmes for SMEs[7]

2.11.1 Financing

Besides the existence of a large number of both local and foreign banks and non-bank financial institutions in Singapore as well as private venture capital funds in the market place, there are two main alternative channels of financing available in Singapore provided by the Singaporean government. Through the two governmental statutory boards Spring Singapore and International Enterprise, business loans, grants and other creative forms of equity or debt investments are available in Singapore for SMEs. The following sub-sections discuss the main government initiatives and assistance programmes available in Singapore to help SMEs develop and grow.

2.11.2 Debt Financing – Micro Loans

Micro financing in the form of small loans called Micro Loans are provided by Spring Singapore to help very small businesses obtain loans up to S$50,000 (or US$37,000). Businesses can borrow to help fund daily business operations or to upgrade factory equipment. Businesses registered in Singapore that have less than 10 employees, with at least 30 percent local equity (owned by a local Singaporean resident), with a company group fixed assets of less than S$15 million (US$11.1 million)[8], and with an employment size of less than 200 workers are eligible to apply. The latter three criteria constitute the definition of an SME in Singapore.

Interest rates and loan structure can be selected to suit individual business needs.

2.11.3 Debt Financing – Local Enterprise Finance Scheme

A second form of loans is the Local Enterprise Finance Schemes (LEFS). This form of loans helps businesses upgrade and expand. For example, a company may wish to automate and upgrade its factory and equipment or purchase a factory or business premises (only for Singapore government owned Jurong Town Corporation (JTC) or Housing Development Board (HDB) properties). Companies that fulfill the criteria of an SME can apply. The loan exposure cannot be more than S$15 million (US$11.1 million) and a fixed or variable interest loan rate can be chosen (IE Singapore 2008).

2.11.4 Debt Financing – Loan Insurance Scheme

The Loan Insurance Scheme (LIS) is a joint programme by Spring Singapore and IE Singapore that help companies secure new loans by insuring them against default. The government will pay 50 percent of the insurance premium. LIS supports both domestic and export-oriented loans such as the setting up of an inventory storage and distribution hub; diversifying into other product lines and capabilities; increasing working capital; expanding into new markets; broadening distribution channels; and supporting and funding majority owned overseas subsidiaries. The types of loans include inventory/ stock financing, structured pre-delivery working capital (including revolving working capital), factoring/ bill or invoice or account receivables discounting with recourse and overseas working capital loans support facilities through standby letter of credit (for export-oriented facilities only).

Businesses seeking export-oriented facilities qualify as long as they are based in Singapore, or have at least three headquarter (HQ)[9] functions in Singapore with a turnover of not exceeding the following: S$200 million (US$148 million) for non-listed companies; S$500 million (US$370 million) for non-listed trading companies; S$100 million (US$74 million) for listed companies; or S$200 million (US$148 million) for listed trading company. Interest rates will be determined by the Participating Financial Institutions (PFIs) and loan repayment period is up to one year. The insurance premiums will make up 1.5 percent of the loan, with 50 percent of the premium payable upon approval of the loan. The remaining 50 percent of the premium will be paid by the government (IE Singapore 2008).

2.11.5 Debt Financing – International Finance Scheme

A fourth loan assistance is the International Finance Scheme (IFScheme) which makes available S$500 million (US$370 million) worth of loans to support companies' expansion overseas. As a credit enhancement tool, IFScheme aims to address the issue of limited access to financing for overseas expansion with IE Singapore bearing 70 percent of the default risk for the Participating Financial Institutions, thus encouraging the PFIs to be more prepared to extend the loans. Loans are available to help companies fund expenses or working capital needs on secured overseas projects/ orders or to acquire fixed assets for use overseas. Companies must be registered in Singapore, have at least three headquarter (HQ) functions in Singapore and a turnover not exceeding the following: S$200 million (US$148 million) for non-listed companies; S$500 million (US$370 million) for non-listed trading companies; S$100 million (US$74 million) for listed companies; or S$200 million (US$148 million) for listed trading company. A company is considered a trading company if it derives more than 50 percent of turnover from trading activities. In addition, the overseas business must complement the Singapore-based company's activities and result in economic spin-offs to Singapore. The maximum loan extended to a company on a group basis[10] shall not exceed S$15 million (US$11.1 million). The interest rates and collateral requirement are determined by the participating financial institution (PFIs).

The existence of such generous funding policies truly shows the pro-business mindset of the Singaporean government towards businesses in general, and SMEs in particular.

2.11.6 Debt Financing – Trade Credit Insurance Programme

The fifth and final debt financing assistance available to businesses including SMEs in Singapore is the Trade Credit Insurance Programme (TCIP) offered by IE Singapore. Companies are offered trade credit insurance at a lower and more affordable premium usually reserved for companies with significant trade volumes. Besides protecting the account receivables, the TCIP also offers financing to meet the company's working capital needs. These greatly help SME trading firms increase their ability to conduct their import and export activities at much lower costs.

Trade credit insurance gives assurance that Singaporean businesses and SMEs will be paid for goods delivered or services rendered. Businesses and SMEs can then offer their customers more competitive credit terms and gain a competitive edge over other suppliers who trade with letters of credit. All these will result in greater confidence so SMEs can explore new businesses and new markets with better surety. Upon verification of the claim, the insurer will pay the SME should the buyer default on payment past the stipulated date and grace period. With insured accounts receivable, the SMEs are also likely to achieve more attractive buying costs and larger credit lines from their bankers.

Trade credit insurance is suitable for companies that are manufacturers, traders, or suppliers of goods and services. The company's sales can either be domestic or export-oriented. All Singapore-based companies are eligible to purchase trade credit insurance through the TCIP. The average premium rates are between 0.18-0.35 percent and companies can apply for TCI alone or TCI plus trade financing facilities. If they apply for TCI alone, 70 percent of the upfront insurance premium will be pre-funded by IE Singapore via an advance. The borrowing company will have to pay the insurance premium and associated administrative fees.[11] Such a policy assists SMEs in Singapore tremendously and once again verifies the findings of Anwar (2004 & 2006) and others that the Singaporean government is indeed very supportive of trade and entrepreneurship.

2.11.7 Equity Financing- Start-up Enterprise Development Scheme

A second category of financing available for businesses is the Startup Enterprises Development Scheme (SEEDS)[12] from Spring Singapore, which is in the form of equity financing. SEEDS aims to encourage private sector investments in early-stage startup companies involved in developing innovative products, processes or applications which can be marketed and sold. SEEDS Capital Private Limited (a subsidiary of Spring Singapore) will match the investment contributed by the investors of the startup company dollar for dollar up to a maximum of S$300,000 (US$222,000). The investment sum by the other private investor in the company must be at least S$75,000 (US$55,500). Both SEEDS Capital and the third-party investor(s) will take equity stakes in the company in proportion to their investments.

Qualifying companies must be a private limited company incorporated for no more than 3 years in Singapore and with a paid-up capital and non-current liabilities of less than S$500,000 (US$370,000). The company's core activities should be carried out in Singapore. At the point of application, the third-party investor (corporate or individual) must not have had prior interest in the company. Corporate investors must be legal entities with a minimum paid-up capital of S$500,000 (US$370,000). Individual investors should have experience and expertise that add value to the startup. They cannot be related to the founders and must maintain arm's length transactions with the founders. At least one third-party investor or a nominee must take a board seat in the startup company. Such equity investments by the state of up to S$300,000 (US$222,000) are extremely helpful for SMEs which may face difficulties seeking loans from commercial banks. Such policies reaffirm the commitment of the Singaporean government that it is really serious in assisting SMEs to develop and grow.

2.11.8 Equity Financing - Enterprise Fund

The Enterprise Fund is created and sponsored by IE Singapore and Hong Leong Finance Limited Singapore, and managed independently by Crest Capital Partners Limited. The fund provides customized financial solutions to companies for internationalization or for export oriented projects, so as to enable you to grow at a faster pace. The funding can be used for working capital, project financing, acquisition financing, asset-based financing or capital for expansion and internationalization. It assumes risk with the business while minimizing equity dilution by exiting upon resolution of the funding concern.

Companies applying need to be established businesses that are privately owned and Singapore-based, should have good management teams, should have good cash flow track records and have at least S$1 million (US$740,000) in annual revenue. The business does not have to be confined to a specific industry nor have a minimum paid-up capital. However, listed companies, start-ups and companies in the research and development stage are not eligible for the Enterprise Fund. This is yet another creative policy from the Singaporean government to help businesses, especially SMEs, and affirms findings of scholars such as Hew

(2004) that policy measures undertaken by governments, especially business policies, are extremely important to help businesses succeed.

For the above equity financing initiative, investment amounts of between S$1 million (US$740,000) and S$3 million (US$2.22 million) are usually structured as convertible loans or debts with equity options and pre-defined repayment tenures. The investment will involve financial participation in the borrowing company.

2.12 Capabilities Development

A list of programmes is also in place to help improve the competitiveness and business skills of business owners, through enterprise capabilities development. More discussion on these programmes will follow below.

2.12.1 Local Enterprise Technical Assistance Scheme (LETAS)

Another Singaporean government initiative for SMEs is the Local Enterprise Technical Assistance Scheme (LETAS) which are grants from Spring Singapore meant to help companies who may require the assistance of external experts to improve their management and operations. LETAS helps to defray up to 50 percent of the total consultancy costs with caps at S$5,000 (US$3,700) for quality management systems and IT e-commerce, and S$10,000 (US$7,400) for IT implementation (upgrading of computer systems or ISO projects). Companies that meet the definition of an SME in Singapore can apply. This grant can only be applied once.

2.12.2 Intellectual Property Management (IPM)

Intellectual Property Management (IPM) is a programme from Spring Singapore that helps SMEs develop a strategy to create, own, protect and exploit their companies' intellectual property. This includes their brands, designs, trade secrets and customer relations systems. Companies also learn how to prioritize their IP according to their companies' strategic direction and how to safeguard it.

The grant can be used in two phases. Phase 1 encompasses IP consultancy projects and the grant covers up to 50 percent of the consultancy fees, where legal and business experts identify the strengths and weaknesses of the company's IP strategy and systems using a tool called SCOPE IP™.

In Phase 2, the grant covers up to 50 percent of the qualifying costs of implementation projects. These projects include IP audit, education and training, intelligence and research, portfolio management, strategy, valuation and licensing. Qualifying costs include costs related to manpower, equipment, materials, consultants and IP rights. The grant is given on a reimbursement basis to businesses that qualify as SMEs. Reimbursement prevents potential abuse of the scheme, as some unworthy companies may attempt to claim for IP related services that have not yet taken place; this demonstrates the alertness and cost effectiveness of the scheme on the part of the government.

2.12.3 Technology Innovation Programme (TIP)

Spring Singapore also has the Technology Innovation Programme (TIP) which aims to encourage local enterprises to tap into technology to develop and improve products, processes and business models. At the enterprise level, projects by an individual SME can obtain funding of up to 50 percent of the qualifying costs. At a consortium level, a project by at least three companies – half of which must be SMEs – can acquire funding of up to 50 percent of the qualifying costs for all its participants. At an industry level, consortium projects that can benefit other members of the industry can receive funding of up to 70 percent of qualifying costs for all its participants. Qualifying costs include: manpower-related costs; professional services; prototype-related costs; technical support services (e.g. testing, certification); equipment, materials and consumables and software costs; and intellectual property rights.

TIP can also help to defray the costs of hiring technical experts (on secondment) from leading R & D institutions such as A*STAR's (Singapore's Agency for Science, Technology & Research) Research Institutes, universities, polytechnics and reputable technological institutions. The scheme supports up to 70 percent of the qualifying costs related to the hiring. The qualifying costs include insurance and medical expenses as well as salary. This part of the scheme is in collaboration with A*STAR's Growing Enterprises with Technology Upgrade (GET-Up) scheme. A maximum of two technical experts can be hired under this scheme for a minimum of at least three months. The maximum period of employment (secondment) supported by the grant is two years. SMEs hoping to qualify must show a commitment to technology innovation as part of their overall business strategy. Businesses with scalable business models and strong growth potential are considered more favourably. The project must be carried out in Singapore to qualify.

2.12.4 SME Management Action for Results Initiative (SMART)

Spring Singapore offers an initiative called the SME Management Action for Results. This initiative basically offers grants that subsidize the costs of developing and strengthening management systems and processes using the Business Excellence framework. This helps add value to customers and stakeholders, thereby enhancing the SMEs' business competitiveness.

The SMART Initiative consists of two phases. Phase 1 involves road mapping. Companies will develop a roadmap that addresses their areas of priority. A designated business excellence consultant will work with the firm to review and identify gaps in the management systems and processes. The consultant will then draw up a roadmap to address these gaps. The roadmap development fee, which includes consultancy costs, is S$5,000 (US$3,700), of which Spring Singapore will provide 50 percent support. Phase 2 involves implementation and review. Businesses will implement the initiatives and review their performance in relation to the business excellence standards. They can engage consultants for help with specific projects. Spring Singapore will provide 50 percent support of the allowable costs, which include manpower-related costs, professional and consultancy services, equipment and intellectual property rights. Such policies are very helpful and encouraging to SMEs, which have ambitions to grow but lack spare funding for business development.

2.12.5 Brandpact

Branding is a very important aspect in business and marketing. Brands stand out as one of the few differentiators in an increasingly commoditized global marketplace. Strong and engaging brands enable companies to create and capture substantial value through premium pricing and customer loyalty. With Brandpact, a joint initiative by Spring Singapore and IE Singapore, companies can receive assistance in the form of workshops, seminars, online toolkits, advisory clinics and grants in various aspects of branding such as brand audit, brand positioning, brand architecture and brand expression, among others. All Singapore-based companies are eligible to apply, including foreign owned companies registered in Singapore.

Such schemes clearly show that Singaporean government policies are non-discriminatory in nature and benefit all businesses, as long as these businesses are based locally in Singapore, employ people in Singapore, pay office rents and pay taxes etc.

2.12.6 Design for Internationalization

Design is another key differentiating factor through which companies can transcend language barriers to communicate to potential customers the qualities and value proposition of their products and services. Companies can receive assistance in the form of workshops, seminars, online toolkits, advisory clinics and grants covering design research, design concept development and design communication, among other areas. All Singapore-based companies can apply through IE Singapore. Such a scheme really proves the point that Singaporean government policy are really creative and innovative in attempting to assists SMEs in all aspects of business as Lawton (2002), Hew (2004) and Neo and Chen (2007) suggest.

2.12.7 International Partners Programme (iPARTNERS)

The iPARTNERS program is provided by IE Singapore and encourages Singapore-based companies to form alliances when venturing abroad. Companies can combine their resources, complement each other's product offerings, achieve economies of scale, reduce time-to-market and pursue bigger projects. This would improve the companies' competitiveness overseas. The iPARTNERS programme assists in the formation, developmental and go-to-market phases of the alliances. All Singapore-based companies either local or foreign-owned can apply through IE Singapore, subject to a case-by-case basis.

2.12.8 International Business Fellowship (IBF)

The International Business Fellowship (IBF) Programme from IE Singapore aims to develop a talent pool with in-depth knowledge of doing business in the supported markets of Central Asia, China, India, Latin America, Russia, the Middle East and Vietnam. It provides funding for

Singapore-based companies to train fresh graduates, executives and undergraduates in these markets. There are four components under the IBF Programme, namely Market Immersion Programme (MIP), Postgraduate Programme, Executive Management Programme and Undergraduate Programme. IBF is open for applications from all Singapore-based companies with substantial headquarter operations in Singapore and planning to expand into the supported markets. The trainees must be either Singapore citizens or Permanent Residents. The Postgraduate programme is open only to Singapore citizens. MIP trainees must not have worked for more than one year in the supported markets.

2.13 Management and Manpower Development

2.13.1 Business Leaders Initiative (BLI)

The Business Leaders Initiative (BLI) is a S$60 million (US$44.4 million) training fund launched in 2008 by Spring Singapore. The BLI runs a 3-components comprehensive initiative to develop and groom SME business leaders. The courses are offered at the Nanyang Technological University (NTU) in Singapore, National University of Singapore (NUS), Singapore Management University (SMU) and SIM University.

The first component is the Advanced Management Programme (AMP) whereby Spring Singapore works with the institutes of higher learning (IHLs) to develop customized and affordable Executive Master of Business Administration (MBAs) courses, short-term Executive Development Courses and other business management and leadership courses for SME managers and senior executives. Courses available include: financing and valuation of SMEs; strategic financial management; creating strategic advantage through technology and innovation; management and growth dynamics of a family business; exit and harvesting strategies for SMEs; competitive strategy for Start-ups and SMEs, among others. Course fees range from S$8,000 (US$5,820) to S$15,000 (US$11,100) per participant for executive development courses and S$30,000 (US$22,200) per participant for postgraduate courses.

The second component consists of a Management Development Scholarship (MDS) which sponsors promising SME executives for part-time or full-time MBAs in local universities. The MDS is jointly sponsored by an SME and Spring Singapore. Sponsored executives will be required to work at the SME upon graduation. The scholarships are for courses in NUS, NTU and SMU. The MDS will provide funding for the following levels: full-time MBA, which Spring Singapore will provide a grant value of up to 70 percent of the expenses including tuition fees, basic stipend and related expenses such as monthly allowance for full-time MBA scholars, and part-time MBA whereby Spring Singapore will provide up to 90 percent of tuition fees and other related expenses.[13]The executives pay only about S$600 (US$444) for a short development course to S$118,750 (US$87,875) for an overseas postgraduate programme.[14]

The third and final component of the BLI is the Executive Development Scholarship (EDS). This is a new scholarship for undergraduate studies at NUS, NTU and SMU targeted at outstanding students with leadership capabilities and a passion to run their own businesses in the future. Successful EDS scholars will have the opportunity to do their internship in Spring Singapore or at a growth-oriented enterprise and are also encouraged to set up their own business.

Upon graduation the EDS scholar will work in Spring Singapore for up to three years where they will have the opportunity to work closely with entrepreneurs and SME leaders, and established strong networks with the Singapore business community. Spring Singapore is offering at least 50 MDS and EDS Scholarships annually over the next 10 years. The EDS covers up to four years of full support for all scholarship related costs, including tuition, maintenance and book allowances, hostel fees and computer loan. All SMEs with annual revenue of over S$10 million (US$7.4 million) are eligible.

2.14 Singapore Workforce Skills Qualification System (WSQ)

The Singapore Workforce Skills Qualification (WSQ) system is an integrated continuing education and training system for working adults, provided by the Singapore Workforce Development Agency (WDA).[15] It complements pre-employment training delivered by schools and education institutions and is founded on international best practices recognized by industries and employers.

WSQ focuses on job competency and encompasses employability, occupational and industry skills. It is a structured programme made up of modules specific to an industry. An individual can accumulate the skills that they need at their own pace towards a series of certifications ranging from certificates to graduate diplomas in sectors such as retail, finance, tourism, food and beverage, security, landscape, precision engineering and more. As an employer, WSQ will help to draw better performance from employees who meet the required standards. The company will then enjoy higher productivity as better skilled employees help to raise the organization's efficiency and productivity.

WSQ benefits everyone including individuals without academic qualifications. This is possible because WSQ recognizes past training, work experience and current credentials in addition to academic achievements. More details on WSQ are given in the following table.

Table 3: Singapore Workforce Skills Qualification System (WSQ)

Type of Training	Conducted by	Current Funding Rates	Current Funding Rates
		Below 40 years old	40 and above
WSQ Certificate/ Higher Certificate/ Advanced Certificate/ Diploma/ Advanced Diploma training	External training providers In-house	80% of course fees subject to S$7 per trainee-hour S$7 per trainee-hour	90% of course fees subject to S$11 per trainee-hour S$7 per trainee-hour

NB: S$1 approximately equals US$0.74 (2010 exchange rate); Source: Singapore Workforce Development Agency

To receive the assistance, companies must be registered or incorporated in Singapore. Training must be fully sponsored by the company and trainees must be Singaporeans or Permanent Residents.

2.15 Training Assistance Scheme (TAS)

The Training Assistance Scheme (TAS) by WDA offers financial incentives to encourage companies to train their employees in areas which can directly benefit their businesses. Funding support is available as shown in Table 4 as follows:

Table 4: Funding Support for Training under TAS

Type of Training	Conducted by	Current Funding Rates	Current Funding Rates
		Below 40 years old	40 and above
Certifiable Skills training courses	External training providers In-house instructors	80% of course fees subject to S$7 per trainee-hour S$7 per trainee-day	90% of course fees subject to S$11 per trainee-hour S$7 per trainee-day
Non-certifiable skills training courses	External training providers/ In-house instructors	S$2 per trainee-day (SMEs can receive S$4 per trainee-hour under SUPER scheme. Please refer to the SUPER scheme)	S$2 per trainee-day (SMEs can receive S$4 per trainee-hour under SUPER scheme. Please refer to the SUPER scheme)
Overseas training courses	Locations within Asia Locations outside Asia	S$80 per trainee-day S$120 per trainee-day	S$80 per trainee-day S$120 per trainee-day

NB: S$1 approximately equals to US$0.74 (2010 exchange rate); Source: Singapore Workforce Development Agency

All companies registered in Singapore or incorporated in Singapore are eligible. Training must be fully sponsored by the company. Workers who are Singaporeans or Permanent Residents can apply. The approved course for funding must be relevant to the sponsored employee's current job and in line with the business needs of the company.

2.16 SME Upgrading for Performance (SUPER)

As a part of the Training Assistance Scheme (TAS) provided by the WDA, the SME Upgrading for Performance (SUPER) provides assistance to small businesses to encourage a higher level of training.

Table 5: Assistance under SUPER

Type of Training	Current Funding Rates
Non-certifiable courses	S$4 per trainee per hour up to 100% course fee
Executive/ Managerial training courses	50% of course fees subject to S$20 per trainee per hour

NB: S$1 approximately equals US$0.74 (2010 exchange rate); Source: Singapore Workforce Development Agency

Companies that satisfy the Singaporean definitions of an SME are eligible to apply. To qualify for executive/ managerial training assistance, applicants must meet the following additional criteria: a) the SME has offered 20 vacancies or more in Place and Train Programme or has employed at least 20 Singaporean workers within a one-year time frame; or b) the SME has developed a training plan committed to the training of at least 30% of its rank and file workers.

2.17 Total Company Training Plan (TCTP)

The Total Company Training Plan (TCTP) by WDA provides funding incentives to help companies develop a structured proposal for training programmes to be implemented over a 12-month period. This encourages companies to adopt a total and systemic approach to training all levels of staff. In turn, this will help companies to achieve their business goals.

Companies can receive training assistance at rates consistent with the Training Assistance Scheme (TAS) mentioned earlier. In addition, external management training would be supported at 50 percent of course fee subject to S$20 (US$14.8) per trainee-hour. To qualify for management training assistance, the percentage of training places utilized by the non-managerial workers must be at least 30 percent or 50 percent for local SMEs and non-SMEs respectively.

As an added incentive, companies may also receive an additional 10 percent top-up incentive based on the total amount disbursed at the end of the 12-month period if at least 70 percent of the overall training places utilized. If the percentage of training places utilized by employees with qualifications of 'A' levels (Grade 12 or Senior High School equivalent) and below is at least 30 percent for SMEs or 50 percent for non-SMEs, a full 'Effectiveness Training Report' has to be submitted to the WDA, to assess the effectiveness of the training.

Companies who are People Developer Certified will also receive 10 percent top-up assistance at the end of the TCTP. The Singapore People Developer (SPD) certification scheme is a national accreditation scheme that assesses if firms or organizations have proper human resource development, training and appraisal systems in place. Training assistance for the TCTP is capped at S$400,000 (US$219,000) per year. This maximum cap excludes the two top-up incentives mentioned above. The TCTP is open to all companies registered in Singapore and trainees must be Singaporeans or Permanent Residents. A WDA officer or consultant will work with the applicant company to develop the TCTP.

2.18 Tax Schemes

2.18.1 Double Tax Deduction (DTD) Scheme for Market Development

The Double Tax Deduction (DTD) Scheme for market development is a scheme under Section 14B of the Income Tax Act of the Republic of Singapore. It aims to encourage Singapore-based companies to expand their business in overseas markets. It allows for approved companies to deduct against their taxable income twice the eligible expenses incurred for approved activities. The following activities are supported under the DTD Scheme:

- Participation in approved trade fairs;
- Participation in overseas trade missions/ market development trips;
- Setting up of an overseas marketing office;
- Master licensing and franchising;
- Advertising in approved local trade publications;
- Printing of corporate brochures for distribution in overseas markets;

- Engaging in other overseas market development activities e.g. market surveys, feasibility studies, advertising and promotional campaigns in overseas markets, design packaging, product/ service certification for exports.

This DTD scheme can be applied through IE Singapore and is applicable to companies with a permanent establishment in Singapore. The business must be an active operating/ trading company with the primary purposes of promoting the trading of goods or provision of services. Applications need to be submitted online before commencement of any business activities. DTD does not apply in conjunction with other forms of tax incentives/ concessions (e.g. incentives under the Economic Expansion Incentive Act and the Income Tax Act).

2.18.2 Enterprise Investment Incentive Scheme (EII)

The Enterprise Investment Incentive Scheme (EII) is offered by Spring Singapore to help start-ups attract investors. This is achieved by allowing investors to deduct up to S$3 million (US$2.22 million) of losses against their taxable income. For a detailed list of participating institutions, see Table 6 in Appendix B.

To qualify, companies must be unlisted non-public companies in their initial years, incorporated in Singapore with business activities mainly in Singapore and have a paid-up capital of at least S$10,000 (US$7,400). The company should be primarily being engaged in innovative and high growth activities, with substantial developmental content for a specific product, process or service. An investor can be an individual or a company. Individuals include the entrepreneur who founded the start-up, and relatives and employees who purchase shares from the start-up at market price (this includes share allocations to employees and shares obtained by exercising employee stock options).

Investments must meet the following criteria:

- Be in the form of a purchase of new ordinary share capital in the qualifying start-up and not replacement capital or debt instruments (such as convertible loans);
- No condition in the shares that would eliminate the investor's risk;
- Shares must be issued and acquired by the investor during the time of the start-up's approved status;

- A loss will be recognized under this scheme provided the sale of the qualified shares is between the start of the second and end of the sixth year from the date of purchase of the shares;
- Each investment must be at least S$1,000 (US$740).

These are extremely innovative ideas which the Singaporean government hopes will entice people in Singapore (both Singaporean citizens as well as non-Singaporean residents) to start a company or business with just a small amount of initial investment (i.e. merely S$10,000 or US$7,400). This government risk sharing platform, through the writing-off of potential losses of up to S$3 million (US$2.22 million) of losses against taxable income, is a very attractive proposition for SME start-ups.

2.19 Other Spring Singapore Assistance Plans

In February 2009, Spring Singapore launched a S$30 million (US$16 million) Incubator Development Programme (IDP) to help nurture innovative start-ups in Singapore.[16] This IDP will provide up to 70 percent grant support to incubators and venture accelerators to enhance their programmes and service provided to innovative start-ups. The supportable costs items include:

- Specific programmes introduced by the incubators and venture accelerators to help startups in product development, financing, market access etc;
- Operating costs, including manpower cost of employing incubator managers and other operating expenses incurred in running the incubator/ venture accelerator e.g. transportation, training, marketing and event costs; and
- Cost of engaging mentors.

To date, Spring Singapore has supported three incubators (NUS Ventures, NanoFrontier and iAxil) and two venture accelerators (BANSEA and Microsoft Innovation Centre).

A new S$200 million (US$148 million) enhanced capability development package known as the Business Upgrading Initiatives for Long-term Development (BUILD) was also launched to help SMEs. More on this initiative to be discussed at subsection 2.27.[17]

2.20 Entrepreneurship Development Efforts

2.20.1 Action Community for Entrepreneurship (ACE)

Even amidst the 2008-2009 global economic downturns, the Singapore government did not slow down its efforts to promote entrepreneurship. The Action Community for Entrepreneurship (ACE), a help group, has taken on the responsibility of remaking Singapore into “a creative and entrepreneurial nation willing to take risks to create fresh businesses and blaze new paths to success”. ACE runs seminars and courses to help motivate and train aspiring entrepreneurs to take risks and try running a business. It is observed that new firms’ formation increased more than two-fold from 11,300 in 2002 to 25,000 per annum in 2008 in Singapore.[18]

2.21 Pro-business environment

As a private-public sector initiative, ACE has made significant strides in reducing bureaucratic hurdles for businesses by working closely with the Pro-Enterprise Panel (PEP) to cut red tape. So far, ACE has helped revise over 900 rules and regulations to make Singapore more businesses-friendly.

It comes as no surprise then that Singapore has earned the honour as the easiest place to do business for three years in a row from the World Bank. Singapore is also regarded as one of the easiest places to get financing, according to the US Milken Institute. Through ACE, the country has made significant improvements in enterprise financing. These include the establishment of the OTC and SME Access Loans.

In Singapore, a holistic approach to entrepreneurship development is being undertaken. Entrepreneurs are recognized and go through different phases of growth, and government assistance policies exist in many shapes and forms to help these business people. At every stage, the needs of SMEs are different and the Singaporean government has gone to great lengths to ensure that the government’s assistance programmes to help SMEs remain flexible and relevant. This is in line with the research by Neo and Chen (2007) in which they both argue that the policies of the Singaporean government are dynamic in order to keep up with the changing environment.

In addition, there are at least a dozen industry awards in Singapore annually to recognize the efforts of entrepreneurs from the 'Ernest and Young Entrepreneur of the Year Award', to the 'SME of the Year Award' and to the 'Woman Entrepreneur of the Year Award.' There is also the 'Business Times Entrepreneur of the Year Award' and the 'Most Promising Brand of the Year Award', to 'Young Malay Entrepreneur Award' and 'Indian Businessman of the Year Award', amongst many others. These awards recognize and help individuals' as well as their businesses (typically SMEs), gain exposure to the mass media and general consumer public and thus, help market these individuals and their business products and services, both locally and abroad.

For start-ups, Singapore has created a conducive environment for growth. Small Singaporean companies and start-ups already enjoy the world's lowest effective tax rates. In addition, companies less than 5 years old enjoy full tax exemption on the first S$100,000 (US$74,000) of normal chargeable income for each of its first three consecutive Years of Assessment. A further 50 percent exemption is given on the next S$200,000 (US$148,000) of the normal chargeable income for each of the first three consecutive Years of Assessment.

2.22 Equity and grants for startups

In the area of financing, startups can tap into funds managed by SPRING SEEDS Capital and Infocomm Investment Private Limited. In addition, startups can also access mentorship advice through the investments of these funds.

Under SEEDS Business Angel Scheme, the two Business Angel Groups play a key role in raising more smart money, to groom more savvy start-ups. With the success of the first two Business Angel Groups, a third Business Angel Group – Accel-X (*pronounced as 'Excel-X'*) Pte Ltd is also launched. This is a partnership between the National University of Singapore's NUS Enterprise (who is an Accredited Business Angel Partner) and SEEDS.

In recent years, more and more young people in tertiary education institutes are taking the plunge into SME startups. In November 2008 "YES! Startups" is launched to provide co-matching grants of up to S$50,000 (US$37,000) to help young aspiring entrepreneurs in Singapore.

One such beneficiary is Mozat, a mobile solutions provider for enterprises, mobile carriers, software providers and device manufacturers. It was first incubated at NUS Enterprise which was then co-matched by SEEDS. The company has also tapped into funds from Spectrum, a Business Angel Group, and also recently received a grant from the Media Authority of Singapore (MDA). In February 2008, Mozat was awarded the "Top Innovator" out of hundreds of mobile applications in GSMA, the world largest mobile exhibition, in Barcelona.

The services that the Singaporean government support agencies such as Spring Singapore provide to SMEs and aspiring new entrepreneurs as shown above, reinforces Wagner, Fillis and Johansson's (2003) assertion that the role of support agencies as well as governments are very crucial. Governments should examine how they could better serve the needs of their SME communities. The Singaporean government seems to be doing quite well in this regard as shown.

2.23 Opportunities for Startups

Further downstream, SME startups can access a number of programmes in order to grow. The following sub-sections discuss these.

2.23.1 Technology Enterprise Commercialization Scheme (TECS)

The Technology Enterprise Commercialization Scheme (TECS), launched in April 2008 provides grants of up to S$750,000 (US$555,000) for innovative high-tech projects developed by local companies. So far, 16 companies have obtained S$6 million (US$4.44 million) worth of grant support under the TECS.[19]

Even amidst the 2008-2009 global economic downturns, opportunities remain for the resourceful and imaginative. During the SARS period in 2003 when business was close to a standstill, SEEDS invested in nearly 40 companies. Some of these companies that the SEEDS programme assisted have grown up nicely.[20]

2.23.2 Enhanced Capability Development package to strengthen SMEs[21]

A S$200 million (US$148 million) Enhanced Capability Development package to strengthen SMEs announced by Spring Singapore, the enterprise development agency, supported some 2,500 SMEs in more than 1,500 upgrading projects in 2008. In partnership with major chambers and business associations, Spring Singapore handled over 142,000 enquiry and assistance cases from SMEs.

In view of the global economic crisis, Spring Singapore's focus in 2009 has been two-fold. First, it helped Singaporean SMEs overcome the current crisis by enhancing business financing schemes, facilitating loan applications and working hand-in-hand with major chambers and business and industry associations to help the companies in their respective sectors. Second, it stepped up efforts to upgrade SMEs and help them build new capabilities and develop markets for the future. What follows is an explanation of the major policies the Singaporean government (mainly through the domestic SME assistance provider Spring Singapore) provided to SMEs in Singapore during the 2008-2009 periods.

2.24 Year 2008 in Review

Despite 2008 being a challenging year for enterprises in Singapore, many SMEs continued to upgrade themselves to seize global opportunities. Spring Singapore also supported over 2,500 growing enterprises in more than 1,500 capability upgrading projects. These projects generated a value-added amount of S$2.9 billion (US$2.1 billion) and created some 9,700 new jobs for the Singapore economy. Some 3,100 loans amounting to S$990 million (US$732 million) had been disbursed to SMEs through 14 participating financial institutions. This represents an increase of 38 percent over 2007 in loan quantum.[22]

2.24.1 Local Enterprise and Association Development (LEAD) programme

Spring Singapore leverages on the networks and expertise of other government agencies, major chambers and business and industry associations to reach out to more SMEs and address their challenges. In 2008, three new industry associations embarked on the Local Enterprise and Association Development (LEAD) programme, bringing the total of participating industry associations to 19. The LEAD programme, jointly administered with IE Singapore, is expanded with a second tranche funding of S$20 million (US$14.8 million) in August 2008 to further support industry upgrading and market development efforts by lead industry associations.

Several new programmes were launched in 2008 to support enterprise capabilities development. These include the Business Leaders Initiative to groom SME leaders; the HR Capability Package to upgrade SME HR capabilities; and the Design for Enterprises initiative to encourage SMEs to use design as a tool for their competitive edge. Two new capability development programmes for the Semiconductor and Environmental Engineering clusters were also launched. These programmes complement Spring Singapore's existing suite of capability development programmes for SMEs.

Spring Singapore also seeded and nurtured many start-ups in 2008. SPRING SEEDS invested in 15 innovative start-ups, bringing the total to 166 to date. The Technology Enterprise Commercialization Scheme (TECS) was launched in early 2008 to turn promising ideas into commercial products. 17 technology projects were supported in the first year.

Spring Singapore's comprehensive suite of programmes has been designed to offer assistance to SMEs and startups in the four key areas of Money, Markets, Management and Know-how (3MK). Many start-ups and SMEs have utilized them to give themselves the additional boost to their capabilities and business growth. For example, local SME start-ups such as Charles & Keith (shoes), Air Market Express (logistics), PLC Industries (precision engineering) and Progeniq (computer software) are amongst the enterprises that Spring Singapore has worked closely with over the years to help build their capabilities.

2008 ended on a sudden cautionary note with the global economy entering into recession. As an export-oriented country, many Singapore companies, especially SMEs, were affected by the weakening global demand. The above mentioned are some of the main core policies that the Singaporean government undertook to try to help SMEs in Singapore in 2008.

2.25 Year 2009 in Review

The Singaporean government has always been pro-business as it believes that businesses provide employment and produce goods and services vital to the economy. It is with this scenario in mind that Spring Singapore plans its strategies for SME development in 2009. Much has been accomplished over the last few years in terms of building SMEs for economic development. Singaporean companies have cultivated a good reputation for innovation, quality and efficiency and Singapore is beginning to see more homegrown companies make their mark in the global arena. Indeed, the 2008-2009 global economic crises presented an opportunity for Singapore's promising SMEs to further strengthen their global positions and widen their lead over their competitors. For 2009, Spring Singapore's priorities were two-fold – (I) to help SMEs overcome the current economic crisis, and (II) to build up their capabilities for the future.

2.26 Helping SMEs overcome the economic downturn

The Singaporean government painstakingly brainstorms new ideas to keep the economy growing during the 2008-2009 global financial crises. The following analyzes some of the major initiatives that were introduced. These examples are yet again evidence of the research by Anwar (2006 and 2004), Neo and Chen (2007) and others that the Singaporean government is dynamic and actively strives to seek positive constructive improvements to the business and investment climate through good public policies.

2.26.1 Special Risk-Sharing Initiative (SRI)

In the midst of the 2009 economic downturn, the Singaporean government through Spring Singapore, helped local enterprises especially SMEs cope with the then challenging economic conditions by enhancing lending and reducing borrowing costs. Enhanced business financing measures as well as a new Special Risk-Sharing Initiative (SRI) were announced during the Singaporean Budget in 2009 to encourage lending and increase SMEs' access to credit. To raise the awareness of SMEs about the various assistance available, numerous briefings had been organized and publicity efforts expended to reach out to as many SMEs as possible.

2.26.2 Financial Facilitator Programme (FFP)

A Financial Facilitator Programme (FFP) has also been set up at the six Enterprise Development Centers (EDCs) and Enterprise Business Information Service (EBIS) to provide financial advice and loan facilitation to SMEs free of charge. The FFP help SMEs diagnose the financial health of their companies and assists them by advising on the financing options and loan applications that the SMEs may require.[23]

The initial results have been encouraging. More than S$265 million (US$196 million) worth of loans has been given out to almost 800 companies since enhancements to Spring Singapore's financing schemes were introduced on 1st December 2008. Among the successful applications, 98 percent were SMEs with the rest being larger companies. January 2009 recorded a high of 411 loan approvals; a 64 percent increase compared to the monthly average of 250 in 2008. Another 140 applications had been approved in the first week of February 2009.[24]

The financial institutions are best placed to assess credit applications. Hence, the government continues to rely on them to make the right lending decision. Spring Singapore works closely with the financial institutions and business chambers and associations to monitor the situation and facilitate where necessary.

2.27 Business Upgrading Initiatives for Long-Term Development (Build)

Spring Singapore is stepping up efforts to help SMEs develop key capabilities for long-term growth by leveraging on a comprehensive set of capability programmes. An S$200 million (US$148 million) enhanced capability development package, BUILD (Business Upgrading Initiatives for Long-Term Development) was rolled out on 1 February 2009 for a period of two years. Spring Singapore aims to support 2,000 enterprises over this period through BUILD.

BUILD provides enhanced support to SMEs by increasing the grant level from 50 percent to 70 percent of qualifying costs for all the existing capability development programmes that Spring Singapore offers. These programmes currently cover areas such as technology innovation, design, branding and business management systems, business leaders' development, process re-engineering, IP management and product development.

BUILD also provides enhanced support to industry associations by increasing the funding support for LEAD projects to 80 – 90 percent. Several associations have been proactive in responding to the crisis. BUILD aims to further incentivize them to develop new markets and help build up their sectors for the long-term. The emphasis of BUILD is on strengthening enterprise capabilities during a downturn so that companies can emerge stronger when the economy recovers.

2.28 Enterprise Fellowship Program

In 2009, Spring Singapore launched more programmes to complement this existing suite of capabilities. Amongst them is the new Enterprise Fellowship Programme which is targeted to help SMEs gain access to local university graduate talents. The programme aims to boost talent development in SMEs by placing and training graduates in high-growth local SMEs.

One key capability that Spring Singapore has been focused on since 2009 is service excellence. As Singapore gets ready to welcome several world-class events, it becomes more critical than ever that Singapore's service standards are up to the mark. Spring Singapore co-leads with four other agencies (STB, WDA, NTUC and ISES) a S$100 million (US$74 million) Phase Two GEMS (Go-the-Extra-Mile-for-Service) initiative to drive this nation-wide effort.

While Singapore is building up SMEs' capabilities, the country also recognizes the need to focus on market development. Spring Singapore will increase efforts in working with EDB, IE Singapore and the associations to help SMEs look out for market opportunities through overseas missions and by linking SMEs to potential foreign clients, both MNCs and SMEs. In the words of a Singaporean government official: "As we face challenging times, Singapore companies, particularly SMEs, must look long-term and continue to 'grow' in business scope and size, 'glow' profitably and 'globalize' their market presence. This will strengthen our competitive advantage, widen our lead against our competitors, and position us well to ride out the storm," said Mr Philip Yeo, Chairman of Spring Singapore.[25]

2.29 Singapore's Global Achievements in the Midst of the Global Recession

Despite the global economic recession which started to hit Singapore at the end of 2008, Singapore continues to do well in international rankings. For example, the Washington-based Information Technology and Innovation Foundation (ITIF) ranked Singapore 1st globally in terms of innovation and competitiveness. Ranking criteria include incentives for companies to innovate at home; being open to high-skill immigration; fostering a digital economy; supporting the kinds of institutions that are critical to innovation and ensuring that regulations and other related government policies support, not retard, innovation.[26]

The World Bank 'Doing Business Report' 2008 & 2009 ranked Singapore number 1 in the world as the easiest country to do business in both years.[27] The American think-tank the Heritage Foundation ranked Singapore the 2nd freest economy in the world in its 2009 report. The annual index measures a jurisdiction's commitment to free market capitalism.[28] The Forbes 2009 Annual World Ranking places Singapore 4th globally in terms of being the best country in the world to do business.[29]

2.30 Recent Government Policy in managing the Recession and Sub-prime Crisis

2.30.1 Resilience Package

The Singapore government tapped for the very first time into the nation's past reserves for a S$20.5 billion (US$15.2 billion) economic stimulus package. This stimulus package, known as the Resilience Package, came in addition to the usual annual budget, which itself was announced one month in advance on 22 January 2009 (the usual Singapore budget is normally announced in February each year). The highly expansionary budget results in an S$8.7 billion (US$6.4 billion) deficit, the country's largest deficit ever. A total of S$4.9 billion (US$3.6 billion) was drawn from past reserves. The funds were used for the Jobs Credit Scheme (more about this below) and the Special Risk – Sharing Initiative.

S$5.1 billion (US$3.8 billion) was used to preserve jobs; S$5.8 billion (US$4.3 billion) was directed to stimulate bank lending; S$2.6 billion (US$1.9 billion) was used for various tax measures to improve cash flow; S$2.6 billion (US$1.9 billion) was used to help households through moves like personal income tax rebates; and S$4.4 billion (US$3.3 billion) was used to bring forward infrastructure spending plus health and education improvements.[30]

2.30.2 Skills Programme for Upgrading & Resilience (SPUR)

Beginning on 1st December 2008, the Singapore government set aside S$600 million (US$444 million) for the Skills Programme for Upgrading & Resilience (SPUR) to help employers and employees during the recession due to the sub-prime crisis. Employers enjoyed higher course fee support for their workers attending courses which are nationally certifiable under the Workforce Skills Qualifications (WSQ) certification system. The course subsidy given to employers for their Professional, Managers, Executives and Technicians (PMETs) staff was 80 percent whereas the course subsidies given to rank and file workers were at a flat 90 percent. The initial S$600 million (US$444 million) was then increased to S$650 million (US$481 million), and subsequently an additional S$100 million (US$74 million) was announced under the SPUR-JOBS scheme, a new two-year programme open to all Singapore-based companies which have not retrenched workers in the last three months. Companies in Singapore can now received a grant of up to S$5,000 (US$3,700) per worker or up to S$400,000 (US$296,000) to co-fund costs incurred in recruitment and training.[31]

Employers also receive cash payments for their absentee payroll under SPUR. Employees also receive training allowances when they undergo their training courses; for workers below 40 years of age, they receive between S$4 (US$2.96) to S$6 (US$4.44) per hour; for workers above 40 years old with 'A' Level qualifications (Year-12 equivalent) and above, they receive between S$4.50 (US$3.33) to S$6.80 (US$5) per hour. The higher skilled workers with diplomas and above can receive up to S$1,000 (US$740) a month while on training. All these measures are meant to help companies reduce their manpower costs while saving jobs; help local workers upgrade their skills or learn new skills that will help them convert to new jobs; and to help employers and employees build capabilities so as to seize the opportunities when the economy recovers.[32]

2.30.3 Extra Loans to Businesses

Beginning on 1st December 2008, the Singapore government also enhanced its business financing schemes to support an additional S$2.3

billion (US$1.7 billion) in loans to help local firms gain access to credit in the economic downturn. The measures will be valid for one year at which point the enhancements will be reviewed for further extension. Up to 124,000 local companies will be able to benefit from the schemes. These enhancements are part of the government's efforts to act early and ensure local enterprises have sufficient working capital and resources to operate.

2.30.4 Bridging Loan Programme (BLP)

The Bridging Loan Programme allows all local enterprises with more than 10 employees will have access to Spring Singapore's Micro Loan Programme; the limit to this loan has been doubled to S$100,000 (US$74,000) from S$50,000 (US$37,000) and the government increased its portion of risk to 80 percent to encourage lending to businesses. To encourage more start-ups, the government also raised the investment capital from S$300,000 (US$222,000) to S$1 million (US$740,000) under Spring Singapore's start-up Enterprise Development Scheme.

2.30.5 Business Angel Scheme (BAS)

The Business Angel Scheme (BAS) was raised to S$1.5 million (US$1.11 million) as a permanent feature, from the original S$1 million (US$740,000) before the economic crisis. The government also temporarily increased its co-match ratio, which meant start-ups will receive S$2 (US$1.48) from the government for every dollar an investor puts into the firm. To help firms venture overseas, the eligibility criteria under the Internationalization Financing Scheme (IFS) has been widened with the caps raised to S$300 million (US$222 million) for non-trading firms, private non-trading companies and listed trading companies. This move is meant to increase the number of companies that qualify for IFS benefits.[33]

2.30.6 Jobs Credit Scheme

Another initiative from the Singapore government to help businesses and their employees is the Job Credit Scheme. This scheme gives businesses a 12 percent grant on the first S$2,500 (US$1,850) of the monthly pay of each local worker. The maximum grant is S$300 (US$222) a month for each worker. The amount is equivalent to what employers would have saved if there had been a 9 percent percentage point cut in their Central Provident Fund (CPF) contribution rate for an employer. The CPF is Singapore's compulsory superannuation scheme meant to help workers save for their retirement and old age financial needs. The grants are made in four payments, given quarterly. The first mass payment of S$920 million (US$680 million) was paid on 31 March 2009 to more than 100,000 Singapore employers who hire more than 1.3 million employees.[34]

On 27 March 2009, a new Business Advisers Programme (BAP) was launched by the Singapore Management University to help match unemployed professionals, managers, executives and technicians (PMETs) with SMEs. The government recognizes that there are many highly skilled PMETs whose unemployment are not due to their lack of skills, but due to structural changes in the economy and these PMETs are a good potential source of advice for certain types of SMEs, especially SMEs with young and inexperienced owners. Spring Singapore will help fund up to 60 projects, paying 70 percent of the S$5,000 (US$3,700) monthly project fee in each case. The SME will pay the other 30 percent of the fee. There will be one adviser per project, and each SME can have up to two projects.[35]

2.31 Effects of Government Initiatives

Since the 1st of December 2008 when the government initiated loans programmes started, government-backed loan approvals doubled in a month.[36] A total of 2,781 loans have been approved since December 2008 till March 2009, with about 90 percent going to SMEs.

Table 7: Government-Backed Loans Approved

	Dec 2008	Jan 2009	Feb 2009	Mar 2009	Total
Number of Loans	226	411	729	1,415	2,781
Loan Amount (SS Million)	80.4	142.2	332.4	764.1	1,319.1(US$722 million)

Source: Spring Singapore; The Straits Times 16 April 2009

2.32 Economic Strategies Committee (ESC) Set Up

In light of the fact that the 2008-2009 global downturns might have been a prolonged one, a high-powered committee known as the Economic Strategies Committee (ESC) was set up on 25 June 2009 by the

Singaporean government, through the Ministry of Finance. This committee is being chaired by Singapore's Finance Minister Mr Tharman Shanmugaratnam and has representatives from various sectors of the economy including the government (9 members, of whom 8 are ministers); the labour movement (2 members); and business and academia (14 members)[37]. This committee with a diverse line-up was tasked to work for six months (July-December 2009) to help brainstorm and identify fresh ways and ideas to grow the Singapore economy in the next phase of development. In addition to the main ESC, numerous sub-committees were also formed and will think of new ideas to complement the main ESC.[38]

Five key areas were being looked at by the ESC namely:

- How to leverage on Singapore's strengths to develop new strategies for growth;
- How to diversify and deepen the corporate sector by rooting MNCs in Singapore and developing local companies;
- How to grow human and knowledge capital;
- How to create good jobs and equip Singaporeans with skills to enable broad-based growth; &
- How to develop strategies to conserve and diversify energy and optimize the use of land.

On 1st February 2010, the ESC announced its recommendations to the Singaporean government. In its report, the ESC recommended that the government raise up to S$1.5 billion (US$1.11 billion) in growth capital for SMEs over the next 10 years, by seeding investment funds set up to attract co-investments from the private sector. The government would contribute about half the amount of capital, and private-sector fund managers would be relied upon to assess potential investments, to maintain commercial investment discipline.

Its several recommendations include setting up a specialist financial institution, similar to the export credit agencies or export-import (Exim) banks in other countries, to support cross-border financing for Singaporean firms venturing overseas.

It is also recommended that Singaporean firms grow through mergers and acquisitions (M&A) as well as through ordinary business expansion. Singapore also needs to continue to attract large multinational companies

(MNCs) while also targeting smaller firms elsewhere in Asia that are now starting to expand overseas.

The ESC recognizes that MNCs are to remain key players in the Singaporean economy as they are major sources of new technologies and allow Singapore to stay plugged into the developed countries' markets, which although slow growing now, will remain sizable sources of sophisticated demand.

The number of Singaporean businesses with more than S$100 million (US$74 million) in annual sales grew to 530 in 2007, from about 280 in 1998. By implementing the above mentioned measures, it is hoped that the number of Singaporean enterprises with more than S$100 million (US$74 million) in revenues could grow to 1,000 over the next 10 years.

2.33 Other Assistance for Businesses during the Economic Downturn

The Singapore government in the midst of the economic recession has developed other numerous ideas of which one is *The BlueSky Festival.* This festival is an event that helps aspiring and promising entrepreneurs start their businesses. The theme adopted for 2009 was *Growth Opportunities in Difficult Times.* Every year has a different theme. Business support particularly in business financing in the form of a S$900 million (US$666 million) allocation is available for the sole purpose of fostering innovation. Initiatives like these are clearly bearing fruit. A study published in March 2009 found significantly fewer start-ups citing the raising of capital as a major issue compared to a year earlier in Singapore. This reaffirms one of the research outcomes of this book that SMEs in Singapore think that access to initial capital is not one of the major problems they face when setting up their businesses in Singapore (more related analysis to come in chapters 5 and 6). Manpower is also less of an issue for these start-ups.[39]

2.34 Singapore's Taxation Policy

2.34.1 Corporate Tax

Singapore has one of the simplest and lowest corporate tax rates in Asia and in the world and this is especially so for new start-ups. For instance, a start-up pays zero taxes for the first S$100,000 (US$74,000) it makes in profits each year, during the first three years of incorporation. In addition, another 50 percent tax exemption is granted for the subsequent S$200,000 (US$148,000) of taxable profit, bringing the effective tax rate of the first S$300,000 (US$222,000) of taxable profits for start-up companies to only 5.7 percent.[40] Singapore is rated as one of the most tax-competitive, business and tax-friendly countries in the world. The corporate tax rate in Singapore is only 17 percent.[41]

2.34.2 Equity Remuneration Incentive Scheme

Under the Equity Remuneration Incentive Scheme, an employee of a start-up can enjoy a tax exemption of 75 percent on up to S$10 million (US$7.4 million) in gains (from exercising stock options or share awards) over a 10-year period, provided certain conditions are met. For more established SMEs, a tax exemption of 50 percent is granted on gains of up to S$10 million (US$7.4 million) per employee over a 10-year period.

Singapore's tax system is very transparent with very clear rules. The filing of taxes is also very easy and simple compared to other countries. The IMD World Competitiveness Yearbook ranks Singapore number 1 overall in 2010, in global competitiveness; in 2010 the World Bank Group also ranks Singapore number 1 among 183 nations for ease of doing business (IMD 2010 & World Bank 2010).

2.34.3 Personal Income Tax

Table 8: Tax Rates for Resident Individuals

Chargeable Income	Rate (%)	Gross Tax Payable (S$)
First $20,000	0	0
Next $10,000	2.0	200
First $30,000	-	200
Next $10,000	3.5	350
First $40,000	-	550
Next $40,000	7.0	2,800
First $80,000	-	3,350
Next $40,000	11.5	4,600
First $120,000	-	7,950
Next $40,000	15	6,000
First $160,000	-	13,950
Next $40,000	17	6,800
First $200,000	-	20,750

Next $120,000	18	21,600
First $320,000	-	42,500
Above $320,000	20	-

Source: All in Singapore dollar. Inland Revenue Authority of Singapore, www.iras.gov.sg

As could be seen from the above table, Singapore has a progressive income taxation system. The highest personal income tax rate is only 20 percent in Singapore, much lower compared to other developed countries such as the United States (35 percent), United Kingdom (50 percent) and Australia (45 percent).

2.34.4 Tax rates for non-resident individuals

Non-residents are not subjected to personal income taxation in Singapore. A non-resident is a person who has spent less than six months in the duration of one year in Singapore. Employment income is taxed at 15 percent or the resident rate, whichever gives rise to a higher tax amount. Director's fees, consultation fees and all other income received are taxed at 20 percent. This is one of the lowest in the world.

2.35 Ease of Setting up a New Company in Singapore

As discussed earlier, Singapore is one of the easiest countries in the world to do business and to start a new business. All an individual needs to do is to go to the website of the Accounting and Corporate Regulatory Authority of Singapore (ACRA), follow the simple and clear instructions there, and using a credit card, a new company could be set up in a few hours' time.[42] It just takes S$10 (US$7.40) and a few minutes to run a check on a proposed new company name and so it could be registered right away. The registration of the company with the proposed directors and company secretary could be done right after the company name has been registered successfully and this just costs S$300 (US$222) and only a few hours to approve. Everything could be done within half a working day, using a credit card and a computer. All the documents could be printed out and filed as legal company records.

2.36 Other Singapore Government Initiatives to Help SMEs

The Singapore government through the statutory board Spring Singapore, has set up an internet multi-agency web portal known as the EnterpriseOne Portal (available at www.business.gov.sg) so that SMEs can obtain information on governmental policies and e-services, such as applying for permits, paying taxes and find market surveys reports etc. For example, it was reported that from October 2008 to March 2009, 79,000 hits were registered on the web portal. The web portal also offers connections to many other services such as EDC's CitizenConnect Centers, IDA's Infocomm SME Programme and Spring Singapore's TIP Programme.[43]

To help businesses cope with the downturn, Google, PurpleClick and the SME Infocomm Resources Centre@ Singapore Polytechnic (SIRC@SP) have joined forces to offer 158,000 SMEs in Singapore a business stimulus package. The package aims to help them attract new customers and grow sales locally and globally by harnessing the cost effectiveness and reach of the internet. The first 10 applicants without a website received one developed at no cost by SIRC@SP. Subsequent applicants pay SIRC@SP a one-time S$180 (US$133) for a website.[44]

At the 13th Singapore Infocomm Commerce Conference held on 20 August 2009, a new Accounting Software Assistance Scheme (ASAS) was launched. SMEs can receive up to a maximum of 50 percent government subsidy when they purchase their first accounting software to improve their financial management procedures. The scheme is part of the Infocomm@SME programme under the Infocomm Development Authority of Singapore (IDA) and would be managed together with the Inland Revenue Authority of Singapore (IRAS). SMEs can purchase accounting software that meets IRAS's requirements and claim a subsidy of up to S$1,500 (US$1,110) per SME, including software customization and training costs.[45]

2.37 Singapore's Workforce Education

In the early years of Singapore's independence in 1965 and her subsequent road to industrialization, Singaporean workforce's educational levels have always been aligned with her industrial strategies and the demand for skills, needed by those industries in question. Aston et al (2002) refer to it as the developmental model of skill formation.

The model consists of three main components. First the state assumed centralized control over their educational systems, in order to build a strong sense of national unity and/ or nation-building. Once these controls are in place, they could be used to deliver the appropriate level and type of skill required for industry. The second component is a clear trade and industry policy which will drive the industrialization process. The third and final component is the innovative mechanisms that the state devises to ensure that the skills requirements of the new industries informed the decisions made about the outputs of the education and training system (Aston et al 2002, pp. 11-12).

Singapore's education and training needs centers around the demands required to support Multinational Corporations (MNCs), industries as well as the public sector. Singapore encourages MNCs to go into higher value-added forms of production. To address the problem of the initial lack of relevant skills by the Singaporean population, the Singapore government introduced the Skills Development Fund, a tax levied on low paid labor which thereby discouraged employers from using cheap labor. The Fund was then used to upgrade the skills of the workforce. However, the MNCs were initially reluctant to fund the upgrading of older workers as they viewed the lack of secondary education as the responsibility of the government. The upgrading of older workers was tackled through a variety of programs delivered through employers but funded through the Skills Development Board. These included the Basic Education for Skills Training program (1983), the Modular Skills Training program (1986) for those in manufacturing, and the Core Skills for Effectiveness and Change (1987) for those in the service sector. In this way the government sought to upgrade the skills of the most vulnerable workers and keep them attractive to employers. Singapore was successful in this regard; by 1992, 78 percent of the target group of 225,000 had undertaken at least one module of the Basic Education for Skill Training program (ITE, 1993).

The Singapore government has also used a similar approach to upgrade the skills of those workers already employed in leading edge companies to prepare them for the next wave of challenges. Working with major companies they have introduced programmes aimed at deepening workers' skills through structured on-the-job training. These OTJ blueprints, modeled on the Japanese system of OTJ, have been developed with major employers in each of the industries targeted for growth and then cascaded down through other employers in the same industry. It was introduced in 1993, and by 1997, over 100,000 workers had been through the scheme. Similar techniques are being used to improve workers' problem solving abilities. Using these and other programmes, the Singapore government seeks to supplement the training provided by the MNCs to ensure that the national skill needs are met.

The other way in which the Singapore government has sought to enhance workers' skills is through the introduction of schemes designed to support the establishment of occupational labor markets (Aston at al 2002, p. 20). Employers in engineering and related industries require workers trained in intermediate level skills but would not voluntarily underwrite the costs of training. The government therefore establishes the New Apprenticeship Scheme in 1990 (modeled on the German dual system), but modified to suit local Singaporean conditions.

More highly specialized skills are embedded in the workforce through Joint Industrial Training Centers, developed in collaboration with major MNCs in the 1970s. The Centers provided high level training in electronics and precision engineering. As labour demand shifts toward more knowledge and technology-intensive industries, their scope was extended to incorporate knowledge from other MNCs and foreign governments. Another distinctive feature of the Singaporean system is the incorporation of labour into the skill formation process. Following initial suppression of the communists, the government has successfully incorporated the Trade Unions into the machinery of government resulting in the National Trades Union Congress (NTUC). The NTUC has been playing a significant role in both delivering skills training and encouraging employers to help upgrade their labour forces.

2.38 INSIS – Singapore Information Services Private Limited

Founded in 1989, the Singapore Information Services Private Limited (INSIS) is a wholly-owned subsidiary of IE Singapore. It plays a central role in helping Singaporean enterprises to reach out to international traders through its various products which span across different media.[46]

Over the years, its stable of both industry-specific and generic trade directories has helped promote the Singaporean business community to other parts of the globe through key circulation channels like IE Singapore's overseas offices, chambers of commerce, trade organizations, and major events in Singapore and around the world.

INSIS's business-to-business portal (www.insis.com) has helped boost its efforts to facilitate international trade and business matching. INSIS also complements IE Singapore's role in assisting local businesses to gain a foothold in overseas markets by collaborating with the statutory board for various publications.

Its brand name furthers its role in helping both clients and non-clients to harness the myriad of trading opportunities available through the world. In addition, INSIS is constantly working with key overseas players to leverage their extensive networks so as to help local companies, particularly SMEs, in their internationalization efforts.

From all of the above mentioned programmes, it can be seen that governmental support in creating an environment and conditions suited for the development of entrepreneurship are very important for the setting up of SMEs. This is in line with the research by Henderson and Robertson (2000) mentioned earlier in this book, in which they found that generally speaking in the United Kingdom, the attitudes of young people towards entrepreneurship though generally positive, viewed that entrepreneurship in the United Kingdom is being hampered by a lack of identifiable role models; poor media presentation of small firms; and a lack of guidance from teachers and specialists on the subject matter of entrepreneurship. The Singaporean government has certainly been working very hard to address all such related issues raised by Henderson and Robertson (2000), and has been rather successful with it.

As much as the Singapore government could boast of the successes mentioned in this chapter, there are examples of recent government policy failure too. One recent such example is the massive paper losses from the Singapore sovereign wealth fund Temasek Holdings.

Temasek has chalked up heavy losses from its exposure to the world's ailing banks during the global sub-prime crisis from 2007-2008. Enticed by the earlier dramatic gains on offer during the late-stage bull market in 2007, Temasek – which is run by Ms Ho Ching, the wife of the Prime Minister of Singapore Mr Lee Hsien Loong - continued to pump money into the financial services industry, even after the first warning signs of serious problems in the banking sector appeared in the first half of 2007.

In 2007, Temasek bought multi-billion stakes in the once mighty Merrill Lynch and the UK banks Barclays and Standard Chartered. The global financial crisis brought along the bear market causing heavy losses.

This fondness for the financial services sector may stem in part from Temasek management's closeness to the bulge-bracket investment banks. Despite the problems faced in 2007, Temasek continued to recruit expensive senior executives from Wall Street, bringing in Morgan Stanley investment bank's Michael Dee in August 2007 and Rohit Sipahimalani in October 2008. The result of the sub-prime crisis was that Temasek's investment portfolio of S$185 billion (US$124 billion) shrank by almost 40 percent by 2008, despite having so many so-called foreign experts.

Temasek also lost its entire S$400 million (US$270 million) investment in ABC Learning Centers, the collapsed Australian childcare provider and formerly the largest childcare company in Australia. The rapid demise of ABC Learning showed that Temasek's poor investment decisions were not limited to the banking sector. Temasek bought into ABC in May 2007 at an overly priced A$7.30 a share, and soon the stock headed south; the shares were suspended at 54 cents each in August 2007, but equity investors lost everything after ABC went into administration because of mounting financial problems.

A second example of a failed Singapore government policy in Australia is the case of the Singapore Power (SP) company investing in Australian's gas company Alinta. Though Alinta has well-established pipelines in eastern Australia, SP's 51 percent ownership in local Australian subsidiary SP Ausnet has been unable to make any gains, leaving SP saddled with huge borrowings.

Another example of a policy hiccup by the Singapore government is the investment by Temasek into one of China's highest profile and perhaps most vulnerable property developers, Country Garden. When Country Garden went public in Hong Kong in April 2007, then the second largest IPO in Hong Kong's history, Temasek joined local tycoons Lee Shau Kee and Robert Kwok as key investors. The company's share fell to half its initial price in 2008, down 75 percent from its peak.[47]

2.39 Conclusion

This chapter attempted to explore the developments of Singapore, through government policy on the societal, educational and particularly on the economic areas of the country. The humble beginnings of Singaporean government policies on the economic frontier were examined. Deficiencies of the government were also touched on, with recent government investment market failures by the giant Singapore investment company Temasek Holdings examined. The list of detailed policies ranging from education to corporate branding, from equity investments in local SMEs to technical assistance schemes, re-affirm the research by many scholars including Anwar (2004 & 2006), Ashton and Sung (1997), Kim and Lau (1994), Wade (1990) and Krause (1987) that deliberate government policies have mostly benefitted the vast majority of SMEs in Singapore and although policy hiccups exist, they are being kept to a minimum. SME policy in general, as in many other public policies in Singapore, are being formulated and implemented only after numerous industry consultations with the respective interested parties such as the business and industry associations, the unions, professional bodies and other related agencies etc. Public consultations are also being solicited through the mass media such as on the television during the regular daily news report, on the radio and also in the daily newspapers.

From the analysis in this chapter, it can be seen that a vast amount of research, planning and thought has been invested by the Singaporean government to cater to the needs of the SMEs in Singapore. It is thus fair for this chapter to conclude that the Singaporean government has done a fairly good job overall, in its policy formulation for SMEs from a theoretical perspective. As a continuation of this study, the next chapter seeks to provide further analysis of existing academic literature in the area of government policy aimed at promoting business activities and entrepreneurship in Singapore undertaken by the Singaporean government, with the aim of linking these policy measures to academic theory.

CHAPTER THREE

LITERATURE REVIEW ON CRITICAL SUCCESS FACTORS

3.1 Introduction

What factors contribute to a firm's success? This chapter attempts to explore the factors influencing small firms' success by reviewing past academic literature in the area of critical success factors (CSFs) and key success factors (KSFs). The chapter will discuss the concept of success from different angles in business from when CSF was first discussed in the academic literature, till the present date.

3.2 Critical Success Factors

The concept of critical success factors in business was introduced in an article in the early 1960s by Daniel (1961); however the article did not specifically mention what CSFs are. The initial CSF concept was vague and received little attention until about a decade later. Anthony, Dearden and Vancil (1972) utilized the concept in the design of a management control system, in which they pointed out that in addition to measuring profitability, the management control system identifies certain 'key variables (also known as strategic factors, key success factors, key results areas and pulse points)' that significantly impact profitability. The factors identified became the basis for the company's management information system and provide the standards for subsequent performance measurement and control systems.

Shortly after Anthony et al (1972), Rockart (1972) observed that CSFs for any business are the limited number of areas in which results, if they are satisfactory, will ensure successful competitive performance for the organization. They are the few key areas where 'things must go right' for the business to flourish. If the results in these areas are not adequate, the organization's effort for the period will be less than defined (Rockart, 1972, p. 85).

Hofer and Schendel (1978) furthered the concept of CSFs by defining (key) success factors as those variables which management can influence through its decisions that can affect significantly the overall competitive positions of the various firms in an industry. These factors usually vary from industry to industry. Within any particular industry, however, they are derived from the interaction of two sets of variables namely the economic and technological characteristics of the industry involved and the competitive weapons on which the various firms in the industry have built their strategies (Hofer and Schendel 1978, p. 77). As can be seen from the above discussion, the modern day definition of CSFs as we understand it today is slowly taking shape.

Leidecker and Bruno (1984, p. 24) view CSFs as those characteristics, conditions or variables that when properly sustained, maintained or managed can have a significant impact on the success of a firm competing in a particular industry.

Jenster (1987) defines CSFs as events, conditions, circumstances or activities, in a "limited number of areas' in which results, if they are satisfactory, will ensure successful competitive performance for the organization (Jenster 1987, p. 102).

A publication by Bamberger (1989, p. 84) finds that the development of a firm's competitive advantage is one of the main components of strategic behaviour, which affects the factors firms emphasize in order to achieve or maintain a competitive position in their main market. Using factor analysis, a total of 26 items are grouped by Bamberger into six general factor groups namely competence and image; marketing capabilities; technological competences and service; financial capabilities; creativity and product differentiation; and low cost and pricing policy which Bamberger calls general success factors.

It is a fairly recent phenomenon in the study of CSFs that a more comprehensive list of success factors in business studies has been derived. Lussier (1995) developed the so-called Lussier Model (as it is known today), a generic success versus failure (S/F) prediction model to analyze the various contributing factors to firms' success and failure. A successful business firm is defined as one that has been profitable in the past three years (i.e. not making a financial loss). A total of fifteen variables or factors are developed by him namely: 1) Adequacy of start-up capital; 2) Record keeping & financial control; 3) Industry experience; 4) Management experience; 5) Business planning; 6) Professional advisors; 7) Education of owner; 8) Quality staff; 9) Product/ service timing; 10) Economic timing; 11) Age of business owner; 12) Existence of business partners; 13) Business-owning parents; 14) Minority business owner; & 15) Marketing skills.

These fifteen factors are identified by Lussier as being important factors contributing to firms' success or failure. This book utilizes Lussier's (1995) definition of business success for a business entity as one that has been profitable in the past three years of operations.

Alternatively, Lau and Lim (1996) define business failure (lack of success) as the discontinuance of business with losses to creditors and shareholders (Lau and Lim 1996, p. 49) and imply the continuation of business with no losses (or having made profits) to be considered as a form of business success; the top six factors influencing business success or failure are: 1) high operating expenses; 2) lack of capital; 3) short-sighted view of the future; 4) lack of control over cash; 5) lack of knowledge over company's products; & 6) inappropriate marketing strategy. Unlike Lau and Lim (1996), Butler and Fitzgerald (1999) consider CSFs as the functions or areas where things must go right to ensure successful competitive performance for an organization.

Ghosh et al (2001, p. 209) define key success factors (KSFs) as factors which are critical for excellent performance of the company and CSFs as the factors needed for survival of the firm. A business has to make at least industry-average profits for the previous three years to be considered successful and failure is defined as not having made a profit in the previous three years according to Lussier and Pfeifer (2001, p. 232).

A previous study by Hopkins (1997) finds that only 3 percent of all small companies grow and according to Feindt et al (2002, p. 51), most firms that do not fail only grow in the first few years after start-up and then stabilize to provide the owner-manager with an acceptable income.

As we can see from the above literature discussed from the early 1960s till the 1990s, the variables that contribute to the success of small businesses are not unanimously agreed upon by researchers. Most entrepreneurial studies have concentrated on a few sets of variables: (1) the psychological and personality traits of entrepreneurs; (2) the managerial skills and training of entrepreneurs; and (3) the external environment (Benzing, Chu & Kara, 2009, p. 62).

With respect to psychological and behavioral traits, Frese, Brantjes, and Hoorn (2002), Hodgkinson (2001), and Olson and Bokor (1995) find that the ability to engage in strategic planning is related to entrepreneurial success. Other psychological attributes such as a drive for independence, innovative orientation, attitude toward risk, and a competitive nature have also been found to relate to success (Frese, Brantjes, and Hoorn 2002; Koop, Reu, and Frese 2000; Dess, Lumpkin, and Covin 1997; Covin and Slevin 1989). According to Frese, Brantjes, and Hoorn, these attributes are especially important when an entrepreneur is working in a difficult business environment.

Other researchers (Rauch and Frese 1998; Dess, Lumpkin, and Covin 1997; Covin and Covin 1990; Covin and Slevin 1989) agree that psychological traits contribute to business success, but they are often moderated by experience and training, specific managerial skills, and the business environment. Since the accurate measurement of psychological traits requires psychological testing, and these traits are often inherent in the entrepreneur's psychological make-up, this study does not attempt to measure or determine these traits in the survey respondents. Instead, this study seeks to determine what other factors the entrepreneurs themselves perceive as necessary for business success.

In contrast to psychological traits, managerial skills, training, and environmental conditions are factors more easily developed and altered by policymakers. Managerial skills would include the ability to manage personnel and maintain accounting records, whereas environmental conditions would be related to satisfactory government support, access to capital, and support of family and friends.

Numerous studies of entrepreneurs in developing countries (Chu, Benzing, and McGee 2007; Benzing, Chu, and Callanan 2005; Benzing, Chu, and Bove 2005; Benzing, Chu, and Szabo 2005; Yusuf 1995; Gosh, Kim, and Meng 1993; Huck and McEwen 1991; Busch 1989) have sought to determine the management skills and environmental conditions most critical for their success. In Huck and McEwen's (1991) study of Jamaican small business owners, three areas are identified as the most important competency areas: management, planning and budgeting, and marketing/selling. Specific competency within those areas refers to maintaining financial records, possessing human relations skills, and establishing goals and objectives. According to Yusuf (1995), South Pacific islanders consider good management skills, access to financing, personal qualities, and satisfactory government support as the most critical success factors.

In a 2003 survey, Vietnamese entrepreneurs selected "friendliness toward customers" as the most important success factor, with "a good product at a good price" a close second (Benzing, Chu, and Callanan 2005). Romanian entrepreneurs rank friendliness to customers, a reputation for honesty, and good customer service as the top three success factors (Benzing, Chu, and Bove 2005). Perceptions of success factors may be partially determined by the education of the entrepreneurs, the competitive level of the market, and/or the extent of government assistance.

In a study conducted among Kenyan entrepreneurs Neshamba (2000) finds that the owner–manager's previous experience, understanding the needs of customers, access to capital, and hard work are viewed as important success variables. Similarly, Pratt's (2001) study of Kenyan entrepreneurs finds the availability of capital, possession of business skills, previous experience, and support of family members are essential for business success. According to a study of Ghanaian and Kenyan entrepreneurs, hard work is considered the most important success factor, with customer service the second most important variable (Chu, Benzing, and McGee 2007).

Ibrahim and Goodwin (1986) conducted a factor analysis of the variables contributing to successful small businesses in Canada and the United States. They find four success factors: entrepreneurial values, managerial skills, interpersonal skills, and environmental characteristics. The entrepreneurial values are psychological in nature and include characteristics such as intuition, extroversion, attitude toward risk, flexibility, and a sense of independence. Managerial skills include variables such as having a niche strategy, an effective budget system, experience, education, and a simple organization structure. The interpersonal skills factor is comprised of good customer relations, good employee relations, and good interpersonal skills. Finally, the environmental characteristics include interest rates, taxes, and governmental assistance.

In another study of small business owners in Pakistan, entrepreneurs rate three factors as particularly important to their success: hard work, good customer service, and good product quality (Coy et al. 2007). Factors that are not considered important are government programs and training programs. In a study of Turkish entrepreneurs, Kozan, Oksoy and Ozsoy (2006) find that business management training and financing are significantly related to an SME owner's expansion plans. To be specific, Turkish entrepreneurs need market information, technical assistance, information resources, and training in finance and marketing to accumulate the resources necessary for expansion.

Clearly there is room for further analysis of ways in which firms, particularly SMEs, can improve their current situation of little or no growth. This book shall attempt to conduct this analysis using literature review and interviews to critically analyze the CSFs affecting the way SMEs run their businesses. The main aim of this study will be to develop an exploratory prediction model that could be used by SMEs and businesses in general in Singapore and elsewhere, to gauge their firms' potential future successes or risk of failure.

3.3 Identification of Critical Success Factors (CFSs)

Though many studies on SMEs, both globally as well as in Singapore, have attempted to identify the CSFs of firms, the identification of a comprehensive list that consist of 'All' the CSFs of SMEs is non-existent, if not impossible to compile.

Cunningham (1995), using six Singaporean business case studies, identifies seven CSFs by which organizations should be assessed: 1) applying new technologies; 2) entering new markets by creating new products; 3) designing jobs which would challenge workers; 4) having a clear vision and direction; 5) gearing policies towards satisfying customer needs; 6) emphasizing career training; & 7) developing discipline and obedience based on an informal atmosphere and professional norms. He finds that Singaporean firms place less importance on: 1) strategies to diversify and develop a range of products; 2) taking high risks; 3) penetrating expanding markets; 4) emphasizing financial performance over other organizational needs; & 5) developing a cooperative culture.

In a study similar to Cunningham (1995), on the CSFs for small businesses as perceived by South Pacific entrepreneurs, Yusuf (1995) finds that the top four CSFs are good management; access to finance and level of initial investment; personal qualities; & satisfactory government support. The view regarding a sufficient level of government support for SMEs to succeed is consistent with the situation in many other countries.

A recent study by Sum et al (2004) looks at the taxonomy or classification of operations strategies of high performing SMEs in Singapore, based upon the key operations priorities adopted by the top 50 award winners in Singapore's annual Enterprise 50 (E50) rankings, a widely recognized ranking of Singapore's 50 most enterprising privately held local companies. They discover that successful SMEs, in carving out their own competitive niches, focus on operation priorities broadly under four categories: cost, quality, delivery and flexibility (Sum et al 2004, p. 327).

Ghosh et al (2001) studies the top 50 privately owned SMEs in Singapore to try to determine their strategy dynamics and KSFs. They find that enterprises need to pay attention to strong market orientation and relevant capability, effective management, strong management commitment and support, strong organizational capability and management cohesiveness and access to broad base support and resources.

Yeung & Chew (2001) research through postage survey 41 local SMEs and interviewed 9 SMEs, in order to examine the advantage local Singaporean SMEs have over their foreign transnational corporations. They conclude that on a national scale, local knowledge and expertise in soft technology embedded in Singapore's supporting industries can enhance the location or 'L' advantage of Singapore. Local knowledge includes familiarity with local technical specifications of products and services, the required local standards, local management styles and the local culture.

In another earlier study, Ghosh & Kwan 1996 study Singapore, Malaysia, Australia and New Zealand in a cross-national study. Their study shortlists 12 main factors that contribute to the success of SMEs including: 1) A good customer relationship; 2) A good service and delivery system; 3) Ability to identify and focus on a market niche; 4) Good product features; 5) A good network system; 6) Availability of financial resources; 7) A good and responsive management system; 8) A good human resource management system; 9) Availability of human resources; 10) Spouse/ family support; 11) A visionary, capable and strong

CEO; & 12) Ability to develop and sustain technological advantage. Constraints to business success are also found mainly in the high cost of doing business and competition. They discover that in all countries, being customer- focused (i.e. having good customer relationships) is the most important success factor.

In another earlier study, DeHayes & Haeberle (1990) find that the most frequent reason for success among businesses is their ability to identify and focus on one or a few market niches. They also identify that most businesses plateau at US$ 10 million and that businesses find it difficult to expand without a change in management style and building up human resources in terms of quantity and quality. Furthermore, they identify the following seven CSFs for business success: 1) The ability to develop and sustain technological advantage; 2) The ability to identify and focus on one or several market niches; 3) Having strong leadership on top; 4) Having significant 'people bonding' mechanism in the system; 5) Strong management team; 6) Strategic alliance with customers; & 7) Strategic use of information technology.

Lau & Lim (1996) study the reasons behind the apparently high failure rates among SMEs in Singapore. Through a survey, they identify that endogenous (internal) factors are viewed by respondents as more critical in causing SME failures than exogenous (external) factors. They view those endogenous factors such as: 1) High operating costs; 2) Lack of capital; 3) Short-sighted view of the future; 4) Lack of control over cash; 5) Lack of knowledge of the company's products; 6) Inappropriate marketing strategy; & 7) Exogenous factor of high taxes as the most important factors affecting a firm's success or failure.

A study on SME business excellence by Hewitt (1997) finds that small businesses can strive to ask themselves the following ten questions if they are to be successful:

1) Do the managers in the company encourage everyone to strive for excellence?
2) Can the people in the company relate their tasks to their overall goals?
3) Is everyone encouraged to improve quality?
4) Do they make the best use of all their resources?
5) Do they know what their key processes are and how do they manage them?

6) How satisfied are their customers and how do they measure this?
7) How loyal are their staff and how do they measure this?
8) What impact does this company have on the local community?
9) Do they compare the way they do things with the best companies in the industry?
10) Do they set and meet financial targets?

Gadenne (1998) attempts to develop a comprehensive theoretical framework in identifying the relationship between various success factors and small firm performance. His study considers the effect of various management practices on the performance of small business enterprises across different industry groups and finds that financial leverage is a common success factor for the various industry groups. He also finds that there are success factors unique to each industry groups such as the 'value-for-money' factor (low prices and good services) for the retail group; the 'good employee relations' factor in the services group; and the 'competitive advantage' factor in the manufacturing group.

Originally using data from the United States Lussier & Pfeifer (2001) develop, a success prediction model with fifteen successes versus failure variables. They test it using a sample of firms in Central Eastern Europe to predict the success or failure of firms via logistic regression modeling. This book adopts the main aspects of their research model including the logistic regression modeling technique and also the fifteen variables used in the research as well as the definition of business success (or failure) i.e. the firm must have been profitable (not making a financial loss) in the past three years; the fifteen variables are the same as the ones in the Lussier (1995) model.

In a topic related to CSFs and firms' performance, Temtime & Solomon (2002) examine the relationship between total quality management (TQM) perceptions, planning behaviour and firm size in Ethiopia. They identify eight critical TQM factors: 1) Managerial leadership and commitment; 2) Customer satisfaction; 3) Continuous improvement; 4) Employee empowerment and involvement; 5) Supplier partnership; 6) Quality culture and philosophy; 7) Resources and working environment; & 8) Measurement and feedback as the factors influencing firms' performance.

Sherer (2003) studies the CSFs for the success of manufacturing networks as perceived by network coordinators and identified eight CSFs including: 1) Participants' character; 2) Chief executive officer support; 3) Confidence; 4) Dedication; 5) Capabilities; 6) External relationships; 7) Intermediary; & 8) Information technology.

Despite the fact that her study is based mainly on the success of networks of manufacturing SME firms, it still provides a good example for thought because having successful manufacturing networks ultimately leads to more business success.

Sparkes & Thomas (2001) list five CSFs: 1) Commitment; 2) Quality of support services; 3) Facilitation; 4) Role clarity; & 5) Co-ordination. These five CSFs are needed for management to ensure performance success. They conduct a questionnaire study on Welsh agri-food SMEs to determine if these companies became successful through the use of internet marketing. A Likert scale of 1 to 5 is used in their study, and is a useful reference for this book, which uses a Likert scale of 1 to 5 & 1 to 7 to gauge SMEs' responses.

In the related business arena of electronic commerce, Tsao, Lin & Lin (2004) investigate critical success factors in the adoption of business-to-business electronic commerce (B2BEC) by Taiwanese SMEs. They single out integrating internet with marketing strategy, top management support, organizational readiness, IS/IT investment evaluation and benefits realization, staff resistance and government support as the main CSFs firms face when they want to adopt B2BEC successfully.

Another e-commerce study by Taylor and Murphy (2004) find that successful SMEs are those that are successful in adopting e-business technologies (for their business success). Factors that are recognized to be critical include owner motivation, experience and management skills; expertise in managing growth; access to resources (money, technology and people); innovation, a competitive advantage and flexibility; close contact with customers; a focus on profits rather than sales; and strong demand and operating in a growth market.

In a separate study related to business success, Hogg, Medway & Warnaby (2003) find that in order for a so-called small business improvement district (BID) to be set up by SMEs successfully, leadership; a genuine desire for change; clarity of objectives; and support from the local authority must be present. A BID is an American concept whereby legislation is introduced for local networks of SME retailers to cooperate to better focus on their local business needs. A geographically similar group of SME retailers can enhance their competitive position by improving the local environment, creating a brand identify for the district and attracting shoppers from a broader area.

A report from the London Business School by Burns and Harrison (1996) identifies six common factors associated with successful growth companies, namely:

1) An experienced owner-manager with a good knowledge of the market/industry;
2) Close contact with customers and a commitment to quality of products/services;
3) Innovation and flexibility in marketing and technology;
4) A focus on profit (not sales) with good management systems controlling costs;
5) Attention to good employee relations, often backed by a bonus scheme; &
6) Operating in a growing market.

Voudouris et al (2000) researches small, little-known Greek firms that are successful and found that their so-called 'Greek Hidden Champions' have four overall strategy themes or 'recipes' for their success. They are: 1) intense specialization in narrowly defined market segments; 2) commitment to customer service and quality; 3) innovation; and finally 4) the existence of strong leadership and a healthy organizational climate. These four factors form the CSFs of successful Greek small enterprises.

In another study on the attitudes of SMEs involved in e-commerce towards process improvement as a part of business success, Jeffcoate et al. (2000) identify eleven CSFs that are relevant to the competitive performance of these small businesses entering the e-commerce market. These include: 1) commitment; 2) price sensitivity; 3) content; 4) convenience; 5) control of processes businesses manage; 6) interaction with customers; 7) brand image; 8) community relationship-building with like-minded individuals or organizations; 9) partnerships with other businesses; 10) process improvement; & 11) integration with other IT systems in support of partnerships and process improvement.

Bliss & Garratt (2001) study 12 entrepreneur support organizations for women in Poland to study the so-called 'best practices' of such groups.

They find that in a transitioning economy, it is important for support organizations to have:

1) A clearly defined mission statement to constrain and focus the founding members;
2) The 'best practices' approach is an effective way to overcome cultural differences and the tendency for members to be suspicious of outside advice;
3) The benchmarked sample should include organizations from countries with similar cultural, economic and historical environments as the transitioning economy;
4) It is important to educate the founding members of the SME about marketing, promotion and fundraising since these are critical to the organization's success; and
5) Initial efforts should be geared to membership growth and fundraising in order to ensure the long-term viability of the new organization

They conclude that the understanding of the social and economic impact of a planned economy on women and the unique needs of female entrepreneurs in the subsequent transition to capitalism are the keys to developing effective support organizations for female entrepreneurship.

Using benchmarking to ascertain the CSFs of firms, McAdam and Kelly (2002) look at SME business excellence using generic benchmarking, an approach defined as benchmarking by involving organizations from different industries. Eight SME case studies are selected by the authors from an initial group of 20 SMEs which use benchmarking. Through a literature review and the study of the eight SMEs, five critical processes are grouped each with an accompanying list of related success factors. The five critical processes are:

(I) Product service and delivery for customer satisfaction (1. Product quality; 2. Services quality; 3. Time to delivery; 4. Customization of customer design);
(II) Customer/ supplier partner identification (1. Product branding; 2. Services quality);
(III) Innovative technology status and benchmark identification (1. Company resources; 2. Product branding; 3. People training; 4. Business development skills);

(IV) People commitment (1. Reward schemes; 2. Training; 3. Company resources); &

(V) Greater production output (1. Employee satisfaction; 2. Training; 3. Capital investment; 4. Service quality).

Generic benchmarking can be done at strategic, operational and tactical levels and is useful for identifying CSFs.

Sadler-Smith et al. (2003) in a study on managerial behaviour, entrepreneurial style and small firm performance finds, through principal component analysis, six broad factors of managerial behaviour are vital for business successes namely: 1) Managing performance; 2) Managing process; 3) Managing stakeholders and the environment; 4) Managing culture; 5) Managing vision; & 6) Managing development. These six factors are important to the success in the entrepreneurial performance of small firms. In turn, the success of the entrepreneurial performance of firms is associated positively with the probability that a firm would be of a high-growth type.

Total Quality Management (TQM) is a management method which has been practiced extensively in business success studies. Sila & Ebrahimpour (2003) study the CSFs behind TQM's successful adoption and find that the following factors are important: 1) Top management commitment and leadership; 2) Customer focus; 3) Information and analysis; 4) Training; 5) Supplier management; 6) Strategic planning; 7) Employee involvement; 8) Human resource management; 9) Process management; 10) Teamwork; 11) Product and service design; 12) Process control; 13) Benchmarking; 14) Continuous improvement; 15) Employee empowerment; 16) Quality assurance; 17) Social responsibility; & 18) Employee satisfaction. These 18 factors are the most commonly extracted factors contributing to whether a firm is able to successfully practice TQM, leading to the success of the businesses.

A 2002 study by Reid et al on successful people management in SMEs in Northern Ireland notes the below factors as CSFs: 1) CEO/director characteristics; 2) Company characteristics; 3) Human resource policy; 4) Staffing practices; 5) Employee development; & 6) Family employee practices. These six factors are the most important factors behind successful SMEs in Northern Ireland. This study finds that the success in human development and people management are crucial factors which can lead to SMEs being successful or not.

Taylor (2005) studies what determines strategic business alliance success in the software sector. Based on the responses of 143 alliance managers, six extracted latent variables suggest that strategic alliance success depends upon a combination of formation and process factors. His regression model demonstrates that the relative importance of alliance process factors is much greater given that they collectively explain 52 percent of the variance in the dependent variable. Taylor's study suggests that the success of a strategic alliance is not necessarily predetermined by the degree of congruence among the partners at the outset, either in terms of their strategic compatibility or relative size and bargaining power. Rather, it appears that the care with which alliance managers nurture the process of alliance implementation is of more importance.

Bernroider (2002) uses an empirical survey and SWOT analysis to identify difference in SWOT analysis factors between micro, small-to-medium and large software enterprises in Austria. SWOT analysis is the analysis of 'key' or 'critical' success factors that belong to the highest ranked set of techniques of strategic analysis used by firms in empirical surveys (Bernroider 2002, p. 564). He finds that the internal variables that influence the long-term success of businesses are categorized into six areas: 1) resources; 2) capabilities; 3) quality; 4) efficiency; 5) customer responsiveness; & 6) innovation.

In a different type of CSF study in 2001 involving internet diffusion in creative micro-businesses, Berranger, Tucker & Jones note a number of factors in the so-called change agents' success. Change agents are people who understand the needs and problems of the clients and selectively transmit to them only information that is relevant (2001, p. 201). The factors identified in change agents' success are: 1) effort in contacting clients; 2) contact timing; 3) orientation; 4) compatibility with client's needs; & 5) level of empathy with clients.

Cagliano et al (2001) studies the international differences in production/operations management practices and successful performance of small firms and makes the following broad findings on successful firms: 1) SMEs need to have higher support for training not only on the technical side, but especially on management issues; 2) SMEs need to foster the adaptation and transfer of principles and practices peculiar to themselves and not just 'pre-pack' existing models from other companies for their own use; 3) SMEs ought to network and foster peer-to-peer relationships aimed at learning and transferring good practices e.g. through benchmarking initiatives. Their full list of variables is included in the following table.

Table 9: The Variables Successful SMEs have in Production/ Operations Management

Manufacturing Practices	**Manufacturing Performance**	**Business Performance**
Strategic Orientation	Operational Performance	Customer satisfaction
Quality & service strategy	Rapid equipment changeover	Market share
Customer orientation	Production cycle time	Employee satisfaction
Quality mindset – TQM	Frequency of priority orders	Productivity
Performance measurement	Process capability	Cash Flow
Integration with customers & suppliers	Internal defects	Return on Assets (ROA)
Manufacturing strategy	Inventory turns	-
Human Resource Management	**External Performance**	**Equipment Management & layout**
Shared vision with employees	Delivery reliability	Flow layout
Employee Involvement	Product reliability	Preventive maintenance
Training & education	Product costs	Housekeeping
Production Planning	-	-
Planning frequency	-	-
Small batches	-	-

Source: Cagliano et al (2001, p. 474)

In another study also on the manufacturing industry, Pun et al (2004) examines the manufacturing sector in Hong Kong and considers the determinants of strategy formulation in this industry. They identify the top five success factors namely: 1) Product/ service quality; 2) Company's strategies; 3) Accessibility to markets; 4) Costs of production/ operations; & 5) Customer services. These five factors are the top five ranked success factors.

Gengatharen & Standing (2005) look at the factors affecting success or failure of the implementation of a government-supported regional e-marketplace for SMEs. The factors identified are broadly categorized into four main areas namely e-marketplace characteristics (technology context); participants' characteristics (organizational context); environmental factors (external or environmental context); and market makers' characteristics. However, this categorization is quite broad and encompasses a very wide area for analysis. As such they are not so relevant in this book.

Lussier (2005) in a study that develops and tests a non-financial model that predicts real estate business success or failure, finds that the so-called Lussier model accurately predicts 84 percent of the surveyed successful or failed real estate agencies, whereas the real estate model predicted 74 percent. The Lussier model explains 68 percent of the variance of contributing factors to success versus failure and the real estate model explains only 56 percent.

A 2006 study by Jeon et al. on the determining factors for the successful adoption of e-business of SMEs in Korea finds that empirical results suggested that the 1) CEO's knowledge of IT/ e-business; 2) the relative advantages and benefits from adopting e-business; 3) governmental support for e-business; 4) using e-business as a globalization strategy for market expansion; and 5) the North Korea factor (specific to the Korean peninsula), affect the successful adoption of e-businesses practices by Korean SMEs.

Benzing et al (2009) studies Turkish entrepreneurs and found that the top 3 most important factors that contribute to their business successes are their reputation for honesty and friendliness; their social skills and good customer service are also cited as CSFs.

Dillman (2000, pp.4-5) tailor designed survey questionnaires using a system called Total Design Method (TDM) and that resulted in high response rates. He develops practical methods and suggests ways that cover each task be it designing, implementing and following up research survey questionnaires. This book takes into account his technique in conducting survey questionnaires closely. TDM is based upon considerations of social exchange theory, i.e. how to increase respondents' perceived rewards for responding, decrease perceived costs and promote trust, and these are applied to respondents in this research. The survey questionnaire respondents and two Singaporean government trade agencies are persuaded that it will be beneficial to them, as much as it is beneficial to this study, to take part in the research because ultimately all three sides (i.e. the SMEs, the government agencies and the author) stand to benefit because when the outcome of the study is complete, it will be published and many people will be able to understand the predicaments businesses face.

Leaptrott and McDonald (2008) assess the relationship between an owner's characteristic decisiveness and the performance of his or her business in a sample of small business owners who started new childcare ventures. They find that decisiveness is positively related to performance. A possible explanation for this is that a somewhat intuitive decision-making process is often adequate; the additional expenditures of time and other resources required to conduct more sophisticated decision-making will then be available once the venture's operations commenced.

A 2008 paper by Camillo et al sums up the common characteristics of successful and failed small restaurant operations in Northern California in the following table:

Table 10: Common Characteristics of Successful and Failed SME Restaurant Operations

Common Traits of Failed Operations	Common Traits of Successful Operations
1. Imbalance between family & work	1. Unique concept
2. Lack of cost control knowledge	2. Generous portion size
3. Too many family members working together	3. Charge only what one needs to charge
4. Excessive cost cutting	4. Sell a concept, not your good name
5. Staff dismissal as an immediate financial solution	5. Standardization of perishable products
6. Destructive emotions	6. Cost and product differentiation
7. Owner's ego	7. Keep creative emotions high
8. Lack of concept differentiation	8. Competent management
9. Wrong pricing strategy	9. Follow industry and technological trends
10. Overextending work commitment	10. Culinary and hospitality management educational background

11. Long hours, no days off, no family life	11. Operations benefits from owners interaction
12. Excessive inventory levels	12. Care for the local business
13. Ignoring technological changes	13. Competitive advantage of new entrants
14. Partnering with close family members	14. Staff seniority in the workforce
15. Little or no investment in employee training	15. Balance price, value, service, and product; appropriate combinations of price/ value, service, product quality
16. Expanding too fast in a short period of time	16. Manage cost, not only revenues; revenue and cost control
17. Disrespect of staff members	17. Balance between family and work
18. Expansion without logical strategy	18. Loyal patrons
19. Relying on personal fame	19. Have a vision, stay focused, act, don't react

Source: Camillo et al (2008, p.377)

Camillo et al.'s study of the restaurant business in Northern California finds that to be successful, a restaurant's business concepts must be: 1) Viable and distinct in the marketplace; 2) Located in convenient locations; 3) Managed with competent staff and management; 4) Maintaining a good balance between food costs and labour costs; 5) Managing employee turnover; & 6) Have service quality and consistency.

Yoshi & Tuan (2009) analyze the regression results of a sample of 337 Vietnamese SMEs derived from a secondary dataset of the World Bank. They find that there are five CSFs: 1) Ownership; 2) Firm size; 3) Firm age; 4) New product introduction strategy; & 5) Competition intensity. These five factors are significant factors for the growth (and thus success) of manufacturing SMEs in Vietnam.

This section attempts to identify the commonly occurring CSFs that businesses in general think are important for their business success from past literature review. The following sections will put together these CSFs into different groups to make the research more meaningful.

3.4 Role of Government Policy

An important element or aspect of good CSFs emerges from the role being played by the government. The existence of good government or public policies that are pro-business is vital for the success of firms. This has been widely noted in past research including Yusuf (1995), Henderson and Robertson (2000), Lawton (2002), Wagner, Fillis and Johansson (2003), Hew (2004), Anwar (2004 & 2006) and Neo and Chen (2007). Good governments create an environment conducive for the development of entrepreneurship, which is very important for the setting up of SMEs. In the United Kingdom, a study by Henderson & Robertson (2000) finds that, generally speaking, the attitude towards entrepreneurship is positive among young British adults surveyed. Unfortunately, entrepreneurship is being hampered by a lack of identifiable role models; poor media presentation of individuals or small firms; and lack of encouragement from important influencers on career choices such as teachers and career guidance specialists. University courses are also found to have their limitations, but are seen to be able to provide a useful insight into the challenges involved in being an entrepreneur, providing skill development and self-reliance.

Tambunan (2005) discovers that in Indonesia, where particular attention has been given to encourage the development of SMEs in recent years, development policies tend to be less successful if there is no concerted government effort towards developing SMEs through cluster development. Businesses tend to fail if this important CSF of clustering is not addressed properly.

Hew (2004) closely examines the development of SMEs and their associated policies in Singapore and the main policy measures undertaken over the years by the Singapore government. His study finds that periodic updates and modifications to current, existing business policies are extremely important, and the public policies towards SMEs and businesses in general need to be explained and future challenges highlighted to ensure the long term success of these policies. In other words, government SME policies must constantly be updated and improved on a continuous basis so as to keep up with the needs of the SME community in the economy as well as the changing requirements of the industry.

Neo and Chen (2007) conduct a comprehensive study on the Singaporean economy and society at large and examine the so-called good governance and good public policies which have made Singapore successful. A detailed explanation on the development, institutionalization and subsequent execution and implementation of the various major public policies in Singapore are discussed. The authors find that leadership, capabilities and change management within the Singapore Public Service are carefully managed, very flexible and highly systematic. Their work reaffirms several important issues, the main of which is that government policies must be dynamic enough to change with the times through the institutionalization of culture and capabilities. This is in line with the findings of Hew (2004) in that positive periodic updates and modifications to current, existing public and business policies are extremely important for a country.

Wagner, Fillis and Johansson (2003) consider e-business and e-supply strategy in SMEs in the Scottish central belt and examine the role of support agencies as well as how a government could better serve SMEs. They discover that there appears to be a short-term outlook on the part of the government agencies, with a dearth of e-business competencies within the agencies themselves. The authors think that SMEs can only be supported up to a point after which they are on their own. This observation is partly true when applied to the Singaporean context. Business firms in Singapore, especially SMEs, are a very fortunate group because throughout the growth of a business firm, from its inception until the day the SME grows into a bigger firm, there exist a whole list of assistance plans and subsidies to help these SMEs in Singapore. These will be discussed further in the next chapter.

A well and established capital market system is also vital for SME growth. A European study by Lawton (2002) finds that without government policy stimulus, the venture capital market in Europe simply will not function to promote SMEs growth because the bridge between the amount of risk and return is too great. He notes that, in Europe, risk capital markets are needed to increase the availability of venture funds because this helps reduce smaller companies' reliance on short-term credit such as overdraft facilities, which is twice as common in Europe than in the United States (Lawton 2002, p. 9).

Fischer and Reuber (2002) make a comparative study of the views of business founders, government policy makers and private sector resources providers and note that firm owners are usually relatively neutral about the value of government backed policies and programmes to assist them; they tend to be less suspicious of government assistance than that of private sector resource providers. The obvious gap that exists between the perspectives of firm owners and external resource providers corresponds to a role that governments are well suited to play. This gap is by itself a critical factor for business success.

The physical location of a firm also potentially determines the success or failure of businesses. Based on a Swedish study of 273 firms, Löfsten & Lindelöf (2002) find that firms located within science parks have a higher chance of establishing linkages with a local university, thus promoting more added values for new technology-based firms (NTBFs). This has important policy implications for the governments because in general, the authors found that NTBFs located in science parks have a substantially higher rate of job creation which is what many countries' governments hope to achieve.

Another policy aspect related to small businesses is that of the dilemma about whether government policy should target support on fast growing small firms so as to maximize its employment impact. Mole (2000) studied the kinds of advice small businesses received from both the government and private business advisors in the United Kingdom and found that the advice given by private advisors are often more risk-adverse in nature, prompting firms to settle for current survival/ reduce insolvency, which is inconsistent with the growth-orientated aim of government policy.

Yet another European study related to small enterprises in six European countries by Dutta & Evrard (1999) shows that European small enterprises have to innovate more, from both technological and organizational perspectives, and build partnerships with governmental agencies and other organizations in order to successfully address strategic opportunities and challenges. There exists a very low emphasis on building links with the European Commission (EC) or governmental agencies and most small enterprises are either not aware of the different ways in which they can benefit from the EC or governmental efforts or are not planning to depend upon such help. The absence of such a partnership is certainly not in the best interests of small enterprises or the countries where they are based.

The presence of 'deliberation councils', a kind of consultative arrangement linking government, business and civil society as described by Campos & Gonzalez (1999) in their case study of firms in Singapore,

Malaysia and Canada, is critical in creating a stable policy environment that is conducive for the promotion and development of business in the Asia Pacific regions. This is the result of effective government policy which can enable businesses, the government and NGOs to meet to discuss any potential issues that may arise from time to time.

With reference to the aforementioned studies and with a focus on the Lussier Model (Lussier 1995, 2001, 2005), a list of general CSFs (variables) is compiled from the most commonly occurring success factors in business from the literature. This book will produce an exploratory prediction model on government policy in general and the CSFs affecting SMEs' success and failure in Singapore. This model could then be replicated and used in other countries for their SMEs or businesses in general to predict or gauge future potential business successes and failures. Table 11 shows the full list of success versus failure CSFs or variables.

Table 11: Success versus Failure CSFs/ Variables

CSFs/ Variables	Description	Recent Studies
1) Capital (capt)	Businesses that start undercapitalized have a greater chance of failure than firms that start with adequate capital.	Lussier & Pfeifer (2001)
2) Record keeping & financial control (rkfc)	Businesses that do not keep updated & accurate records and do not use adequate financial controls have a greater chance of failure than firms that do.	Lussier & Pfeifer (2001)
3) Industry Experience (inex)	Businesses managed by people without prior industry experience have a greater chance of failure than firms managed by people with prior industry experience.	Lussier & Pfeifer (2001)
4) Management Experience (maex)	Businesses managed by people without prior management experience have a greater chance of failure than firms managed by people with prior management experience.	Lussier & Pfeifer (2001)

5) Planning (plan)	Businesses that do not develop specific business plans have a greater chance of failure than firms that do.	Lussier & Pfeifer (2001)
6) Professional Advisors (prad)	Businesses that do not use professional advisors have a greater chance of failure than firms using professional advisors. A more recent source of professional advisors is venture capitalists.	Lussier & Pfeifer (2001)
7) Education (educ)	People without university education who start a business have a greater chance of failure than people with one or more years of university education.	Lussier & Pfeifer (2001)
8) Staffing (staff)	Businesses that cannot attract and retain quality employees have a greater chance of failure than firms that can.	Lussier & Pfeifer (2001)
9) Product/ Service Timing (psti)	Businesses that select products/services that are too new or too old have a greater chance of failure than firms that select products/services that are in the growth stage.	Lussier & Pfeifer (2001)
10) Economic Timing (ecti)	Businesses that start during a recession have a greater chance of failure than firms that start during expansion periods.	Lussier & Pfeifer (2001)
11) Age (age)	Younger people who start a business have a greater chance of failure than older people starting a business.	Lussier & Pfeifer (2001)
12) Partners (part)	A business started by one person has a greater chance of failure than a firm started by more than one person.	Lussier & Pfeifer (2001)

13) Parents (pent)	Business owners whose parents did not own a business have a greater chance of failure than owners whose parents did own a business.	Lussier & Pfeifer (2001)
14) Minority (mior)	Business owners who are ethnic minorities have a greater chance of failure than non-minorities.	Lussier & Pfeifer (2001)
15) Marketing (mrkt)	Business owners without marketing skills have a greater chance of failure than owners with marketing skills	Lussier & Pfeifer (2001)
16) Good Customer Relations (rela)	Businesses with not-so-good customers' relations have a higher chance of failure than those with good customer relations	Ghosh et al (2001); Ghosh & Kwan (1996)
17) Niches Market (Niche)	Businesses without a niche market will have a higher chance of failure than those with a niche market	Ghosh et al (2001); DeHayes & Haeberle (1990)
18) High Cost of Doing Business (cost)	Business with high costs of doing business have a higher chance of failure than those with lower costs of doing business	Ghosh & Kwan (1996)
19) Ability to Develop & Sustain technology edge (tech)	Businesses that have the ability to develop & sustain their technology edge will have a better chance of success than those without the ability	DeHayes & Haeberle (1990)
20) Competition (Compete)	Businesses with strong competition from competitors will have a higher chance of failure than those without/ less competition	Ghosh & Kwan (1996)
21) Strong Top Leadership (Lead)	Businesses with strong top leadership will have a higher chance of success than those without strong leadership	Ghosh et al (2001); DeHayes & Haeberle (1990); Ghosh & Kwan (1996)

22) Significant 'People bonding' in firm (PeoBond)	Businesses with significant 'people bonding' will have a higher chance of success than those without 'people bonding'	DeHayes & Haeberle (1990)
23) Strong Organizational Capability (Org Cap)	Businesses with strong organizational capability will have a higher chance of success than those without strong organizational capability	Ghosh et al (2001)
24) Access to broad Support & Resources (Broad Access)	Businesses with good access to a broad range of support and resources will have a higher chance of success than those without good access	Ghosh et al (2001)
25) Local Knowledge (LKnow)	Businesses with good local knowledge of the local business environment will have a higher chance of success than those without good local knowledge	Yeung & Chew (2001)
26) Government Policy (govt)	Existence of good government policies will increase the chance of businesses succeeding than without good government policies	Ghosh et al (2001)

Source: Teng, Bhatia & Anwar (2011)

3.5 Knowledge Gap

Despite the fact that government policies and CSFs are widely studied in areas around the world including in Singapore, there is no comprehensive prediction model available to test if firms have potential to be successful or are more prone to failures. Much research investigates the non-financial factors contributing to success versus failure of small firms, but empirical tests of the predictability of these factors are less common. This book, which is primarily quantitative/ positivist in nature will attempt to fill this gap.

3.6 Conclusion

This chapter attempted to define the concept of critical success factors by reviewing past academic literature in the area of CSFs and also the closely related key success factors (KSFs). It demonstrated how the concept or perception of success has changed from the early days when CSFs were first discussed in the academic literature, till the present day. The next chapter will discuss the research methodology of this book.

CHAPTER FOUR

RESEARCH METHODOLOGY

4.1 Introduction

This chapter will discuss about the research techniques which this book uses. Specifically, it will outline the research design and methodology which this book adopts and the rationale behind their usage. The choice of survey questionnaires and interviews and the design of questions for the questionnaires and interviews are discussed and methods analysis of the data collected are discussed.

4.2 Research Design & Methodology

Firstly, self-administered online survey questionnaires (Yeung & Chew 2001, p.436) were emailed to SME businesses in Singapore, through different trade and business associations' internet listed business directories. This method is able to accurately gauge the attitudes and sentiments of SMEs businesses and reduce potential common method variance (Tharenou et al 2007, p. 62). A system of scoring was employed to make the survey questionnaire results quantitative for use in logistic regression and factor reduction analysis. It is assumed that local SME respondents are truthful in answering the stipulated questions. It is also assumed that responding SMEs are currently in operation/ in business and not facing bankruptcy or other financial or business problems. Only SMEs that define themselves as successful/ unsuccessful, were included in the survey i.e. SMEs which have made at least industry-average profits or a loss in the last three years are included in this book. A question in the questionnaire was included to ascertain this criterion.

Secondly, from the side of the government, as far as government SME policies are concerned, appointments to interview (Yeung & Chew 2001) one senior person from each of the following government statutory bodies namely: Spring Singapore[48], International Enterprise Singapore (IE)[49] and the Economic Development Board of Singapore (EDB)[50] were made.

These three organizations are government related organizations which execute, provide assistance and advise SMEs about, SME related policies in Singapore. Though substantial SME information can be found in existing publicly available avenues (e.g. websites, annual reports etc), interviewing a senior person from each of the aforementioned government bodies gives a more updated picture of any new policies that are in place or that may be implemented soon. Permission was sought to tape record the interviews for better analysis. However, only IE Singapore allowed this; Spring Singapore declined, stating that it is their organization's policy not to be on record for such interviews.

Both IE Singapore and Spring Singapore were successfully interviewed. EDB replied via email that their portfolio no longer included the promotion of SMEs in Singapore. EDB's responsibility now is mainly pursuing and promoting foreign direct investment (FDI) in Singapore.

4.2.1 Survey Questionnaire

This book formulated 35 specific questions to probe the SMEs to ascertain the state of their business operations and also determine if the SMEs think Singaporean government policies for small business have been beneficial. Survey questionnaires were sent via email to the listed email addresses of members of the business associations (The survey questionnaire is attached in Appendix D). All the responses were given a scoring/ points system (i.e. 1 to 7 or 1 to 5, as shown in Appendix D), which was used to gauge the sentiments of SMEs. These scores were then used to run regressions to test the hypotheses outlined in Section 1.3.

The respondents are SMEs who are members of business associations; members of chambers of commerce and industries in Singapore; or listed businesses in the 2009 edition of the publication *Singapore SME 500* and the 2008/2009 edition of the Singapore Yellow Pages (Buying Guide). A quantitative study was used because it is the most suitable method to subsequently run logistic regression model tests and to test the statistical significance of the hypotheses.

4.2.2 Interviews

Interviews with a representative from the two relevant government statutory bodies Spring Singapore, International Enterprises Singapore were also conducted. These two interviews provide an update of recent

SME policies and also give a background and the history of the development of SME policy. These are extremely important and useful in understanding Singapore's public and government policy on SMEs, in addition to reading existing available literature on current policies (Tharenou et al 2007 pp. 102-122).

The interviews with the two government statutory bodies provided a first-hand account of the latest or new government initiatives aimed at helping SMEs and promoting their growth.

4.3 Instruments and Measurements

4.3.1 Questionnaire Design and Measurements

The data collection methodology of this book involved self-administered questionnaires (Tharenou 2007, pp. 101-121) whereby the target respondents were a senior staff (proprietor/Chairperson/MD/CEO/director or senior manager) of the SMEs. Survey emails were sent to these organizations, through the above mentioned business associations, requesting them to disseminate to their members. A total of about three months had been taken for the entire interviews to be conducted, and the dissemination and return/ collection of the survey questionnaires. Dillman (2000) is also referred to, in an attempt to increase participation rates.

Crotty (1998) uses the metaphor of a building scaffolding to create an image of the research process and emphasizes two core questions that underpin the focus of the investigation namely: (1) what methodology and methods will be used; (2) how are these choices explained, justified and defended?

Data collection using web-based online survey questionnaires is one of the most simple and cost effective research survey methods nowadays. 35 questions were designated in the questionnaire (an estimated 5-10 minutes questionnaire filling time). Besides sending the initial first email to the business associations' general business enquiry email address, their listed members were also e-mailed directly; the latter method is more personalized and may encourage more people to respond. All the questions used in the online survey questionnaires were exactly the same.

4.3.2 Question Design

A total of 35 questions were used because too many questions or too long an interview or survey questionnaire may put potential respondents off. Introductory letters & questionnaires were sent by email and conventional mail where hard copies of the questionnaires can be sent with self-addressed prepaid postage if the target respondents expressed a preference for this mode of survey (Cavana, Delahaye & Sekaran 2001, p. 243). However, no SME requested this method. The entire island of Singapore was covered randomly as business associations' members are located anywhere around Singapore.

In addition, direct telephone cold calls requesting 5-10 minutes of time from a senior person or manager in-charge of (specific random area mapping TBA) were also conducted because the number of initial online respondents turned out to be low. Verbal permission/ agreement from the senior management staff was sought before the telephone survey started.

4.3.3 Likert Scale

A points or scoring system (1 to 7; 1 for strongly agree, 7 for strongly disagree) was used to convert the results of the completed returned survey questionnaires into quantitative numerical figures, so as to be able to subsequently run regressions to test the hypotheses (Tharenou et al 2007, pp. 179-185). The scoring system is as follows:

1) Strongly Agree
2) Agree
3) Somewhat Agree
4) Neutral/ Can't Tell
5) Somewhat Disagree
6) Disagree
7) Strongly Disagree

SPSS is used for analyzing whether the outcomes from the respondents support the hypothesis/ proposition that successful/ failing SMEs possess the criteria of the various variables or CSFs. A copy of the questions (with a points/ scoring system) is provided in the appendices.

A 'feel of the collected data' was gathered during the pre-testing referred to earlier in Section 4.4 to ensure that the questions in the interviews and survey questionnaire made sense, and to see if any biases exist. No such problems were identified.

4.3.4 Questions in Survey Questionnaire

The 35 questions in the online survey questionnaire aim to survey the attitudes of SMEs in Singapore about the issue of whether good government policy and a specific set of CSFs exist for the successful running of their businesses.

Questions 1,2, and 29-35 measure the fundamental conditions associated with the definitions of an SME business in Singapore, and attempt to also survey the type of industry (i.e. services, manufacturing, agriculture) the responding SMEs are engaged in, along with their company assets, average annual sales and percentage of sales meant for export.

Questions 3-28 measure the 26 variables which attempt to study the CSFs of the businesses. As mentioned earlier, the 26 variables (or factors) are:

1) SME having sufficient capital when started (capt);
2) SME keeping good business and financial records (rkfc);
3) SME owner(s) having past industry experience (inex);
4) SME owner(s) having past management experience (maex);
5) SME has a specific business plan (plan);
6) SME having professional advisors (prad);
7) SME being run by people with university education (educ);
8) SME being able to retain good staff (staff);
9) SME having very new or very old products/ services (psti);
10) SME started in an economic boom or recession (ecti);
11) Age of the SME owner(s) when the firm started (age);
12) Number of business partner(s) in the SME (part);
13) SME owner(s) having parents who were business people (pent);
14) SME owner(s) is/ are an ethnic minority (mior);
15) SME owner(s) having past marketing skills (mrkt);
16) SME has good customer/ business relationships (rela);
17) SME has good niche market(s) (Niches);
18) SME has high business costs (Cost);
19) SME has ability to develop & sustain technology edge (tech);
20) SME having strong competitors (compete);
21) SME has strong top leadership (Lead);
22) SME has strong people bonding (PeoBond);

23) SME has strong organizational capability (OrgCap);
24) SME has access to broad support & resources (BroadAccess);
25) SME has good local knowledge of market (LKnow); &
26) SME believes good government policy exists for SMEs (govt).

The above variables are then analyzed using two main analysis methods namely: 1) Logistic regression modeling; & 2) Principal component analysis.

4.3.5 Categorization of Variables into Groups

Yusuf (1995) performed factor analysis and grouped the variables into four distinct groupings namely: 1) Good management; 2) Access to finance and initial level of investment; 3) Personal qualities; & 4) Government support. Taking the approach of Yusuf (1995) into consideration with slight modification, this book grouped the variables into the below six models:

1. Model 1: Full 26 variable Exploratory Model (variables: capt; rkfc; inex; maex; plan; prad; educ; staff; pcti; ecti; age; part; pent; mrkt; mior; rela; niche; cost; tech; compete; lead; peobond; orgcap; broadaccess; lknow; govt)
2. Model 2: Good management (8 variables: rkfc; inex; maex; plan; educ; mrkt; Lead; orgcap)
3. Model 3: Access to finance & level of initial investment (1 variable: capt);
4. Model 4: Personal qualities (16 variables: prad; staff; psti; ecti; age; part; pent; mior; rela; niche; cost; tech; compete; Peobond; BroadAccess; LKnow)
5. Model 5: Government Support (1 variable: govt)
6. Model 6: The 15 variable original Lussier Model (15 variables: capt; rkfc; inex; maex; plan; prad; educ; staff; pcti; ecti; age; part; pent; mior; mrkt)

The above four distinct grouping of variables (Models 2, 3, 4 &5) by Yusuf (1995) appear to be the most suitable for this study and were adopted together with the 26-variable Exploratory Model and 16-variable Lussier Model. Subsequently, factor analysis is used to group the variables with similar characteristics together into various groups. With factor analysis, a smaller number of factors can be produced from a large number of variables which will then be capable of explaining the observed variance in the larger number of variables. The reduced factors can then be used for further analysis.

4.3.6 Reliability & Validity of Data and Research

Reliability is concerned with how much random error there is in the measurement of a variable (Tharenou et al 2007, pp. 24-25). Survey responses were scoured for any tell-tale signs or signals that may suggest that the respondents are not serious when answering the online survey questionnaires such as constantly selecting one single choice (number) that does not make any sense (e.g. always selecting choice number 1 or any other particular number) while answering the questionnaires (Seidman 2006, pp. 22-27). The interviews with the two government statutory bodies are assumed to be reliable, as they are national statutory organizations (of high social/ public standing in Singapore). The results from those respondents found not to be serious are not used. A Cronbach's Alpha value of 0.7 or greater implies that the data is of a reliable quality.

Validity is concerned with whether the researcher is measuring the construct he purports to be measuring (Donohue et al 2007, pp. 24-27); that is the extent to which the measure measures what it is supposed to measure. Maxwell (2005, p. 105) mentioned 'validity is not a commodity that can be purchased with techniques…it depends on the relationship of your conclusions to reality and there are no methods that can completely assure that you have captured this.'

The reliability analysis function of SPSS is also used to study the properties of the measurement scales and the items that make them up; all items with Alpha values of 0.7 and above will be acceptable (Tharenou et al 2007, p. 153). The Reliability Analysis procedure calculates a number of commonly used measures of scale reliability and also provides information about the relationships between individual items in the scale. Intra-class correlation coefficients can be used to compute inter-rater reliability estimates (SPSS 13.0 Base User's Guide 2004, p. 537).

A question that needs to be asked is "Did the questions in the questionnaires measure SMEs attitude in a useful way?" Using reliability analysis from SPSS, the extent to which the items in the questionnaires are related to each other was determined, to get an overall index of the repeatability or internal consistency of the scale as a whole, and identify problem items that should be excluded from the research.

4.3.7 Non-Response Bias

With regards to non-response bias, one method of testing for non-response bias is to use late respondents as surrogates for non-respondents (Lussier & Pfeifer 2001, p. 233). The responses of the early respondents are contrasted with those of the respondents who responded late (e.g. after my follow-up call/ email) to see if any responses are significantly different between the two groups using t and chi-square tests. There are no significant differences ($p < 0.05$), which suggests that no systematic non-response bias that will affect the results.

In addition, the secondary method of directly telephoning the respondents also helped reduce potential non-response bias (if only using the first online survey method) as well as common method variance.

A total of 176 survey replies are collected. The results of the pre-tests and pilot tests were analysed to seek the opinions of the test respondents about whether the survey questionnaire's face validity, content validity etc among others, made sense. Care has been taken to ensure that the research is valid and reliable, and conceptually sound.

4.3.8 Key Variables

From the review of recent literature, six business prediction models consisting of the following are gathered for analysis:

a) Model 1 (26 variables) aka the Exploratory Model;
b) Model 2 (8 variables) aka the Good Management Model;
c) Model 3 (1 variable) aka the Access to Finance Model;
d) Model 4 (16 variables) aka the Personal Qualities Model;
e) Model 5 (1 variable) aka the Good Government Model; &
f) Model 6 (15 variables) aka the Lussier Model.

These six models are broadly grouped together to allow a comparison between them. This is done in accordance with past research by Yusuf (1995) in which he grouped business success variables into four distinct groups namely: good management; access to finance and initial level of investment; (firm's unique) personal qualities; & government support. This book goes one step further by introducing the 26 variable Exploratory Model (Model 1) and also the 15 variable Lussier (1995) Model (Model 2) as a control model. More on these comparisons will be discussed in chapters 5 and 6. These variables are the most commonly occurring factors in the literature on CSFs for businesses from around the world. The dependent variable is dichotomous: either business success or failure. The independent variables are the CSFs of businesses. All the six models are compiled from the literature review.

Table 12: Good Management Model (8 variables)

CSFs/ Variables	**Description & Recent Studies Done**
1) Record keeping & financial control (rkfc)	Businesses that do not keep updated & accurate records and do not use adequate financial controls have a greater chance of failure than firms that do. Recent studies: Lussier & Pfeifer (2001); Hewitt (1997); Lau & Lim (1996); Huck & McEwen (1991); Ibrahim & Goodwin (1986)
2) Industry Experience (inex)	Businesses managed by people without prior industry experience have a greater chance of failure than firms managed by people with prior industry experience. Recent studies: Lussier & Pfeifer (2001); Neshamba (2000); Burns & Harrison (1996)
3) Management Experience (maex)	Businesses managed by people without prior management experience have a greater chance of failure than firms managed by people with prior management experience. Recent studies: Benzing, Chu & Kara (2009); Kozan, Oksay & Ozsay (2006); Lussier & Pfeifer (2001); Yeung & Chew (2001); Neshamba (2000); Rauch & Frese (1998); Dess, Lumpkin & Covin (1997); Gosh, Kim & Meng (1993); Huck & McEwen (1991); Covin & Covin

	(1990); Covin & Slevin (1989); Ibrahim & Goodwin (1986)
4) Planning (plan)	Businesses that do not develop specific business plans have a greater chance of failure than firms that do. Recent studies: Frese, Brantjes & Hoorn (2002); Hodgkinson (2001); Lussier & Pfeifer (2001); Olson & Bokor (1995); Huck & McEwen (1991)
5) Education (educ)	People without university education who start a business have a greater chance of failure than people with one or more years of university education. Recent studies: Lussier & Pfeifer (2001)
6) Marketing (mrkt)	Business owners without marketing skills have a greater chance of failure than owners with marketing skills. Recent studies: Lussier & Pfeifer (2001); Lau & Lim (1996); Huck & McEwen (1991); Bamberger (1989)
7) Strong Top Leadership (Lead)	Businesses with strong top leadership will have a higher chance of success than those without strong leadership. Recent studies: Camillo (2008); Hogg, Medway & Warnaby (2003); Ghosh et al (2001); Temtime & Solomon (2002) ; Voudouris et al (2000) ; Ghosh & Kwan (1996); DeHayes & Haeberle (1990)
8) Strong Organizational Capability (Org Cap)	Businesses with strong organizational capability will have a higher chance of success than those without strong organizational capability. Recent studies: Ghosh et al (2001)

Table 12 shows the good management model which consist of eight CSFs. With reference to the table, an SME with good senior management staff generally speaking ought to have good business record keeping and financial control systems in place; have relevant past industry experience; relevant past management experience; the firm ought to have a proper business plan in place; the business owner ought to have a good university education; have good marketing skills because almost any kinds of business have goods or services to sell; have good top leaders in the firm; & the senior management ought to have good organizational capabilities.

Table 13: Access to Finance Model (1 variable)

CSF/ Variable	Description & Recent Studies Done
1) Capital (capt)	Businesses that start undercapitalized have a greater chance of failure than firms that start with adequate capital. Recent studies: Kozan, Oksay & Ozsay (2006); Lussier & Pfeifer (2001); Ghosh (2001); Pratt (2000); Neshamba (2000); Gadenne (1998); Lau & Lim (1996); Yusuf (1995); Bamberger (1986)

Table 13 shows the Access to Finance Model which consists of 1 CSF. Having sufficient setup capital and an initial level of investment is extremely important for any SME. Without enough capital, many SMEs will usually not last very long, especially during the initial years of operation when businesses have yet to take off.

Table 14: Personal Qualities Model (16 variables)

CSFs/ Variables	Description & Recent Studies Done
1) Professional Advisors (prad)	Businesses that do not use professional advisors have a greater chance of failure than firms using professional advisors. A more recent source of professional advisors is venture capitalists. Recent studies: Lussier & Pfeifer (2001)

2) Staffing (staff)	Businesses that cannot attract and retain quality employees have a greater chance of failure than firms that can. Recent studies: Camillio (2008); Lussier & Pfeifer (2001); Ghosh (2001); Gadenne (1998); Hewitt (1997); DeHayes & Haeberle (1990)
3) Product/ Service Timing (psti)	Businesses that select products/services that are too new or too old have a greater chance of failure than firms that select products/services that are in the growth stage. Recent studies: Lussier & Pfeifer (2001)
4) Economic Timing (ecti)	Businesses that start during a recession have a greater chance of failure than firms that start during expansion periods. Recent studies: Lussier & Pfeifer (2001)
5) Age (age)	Younger people who start a business have a greater chance of failure than older people starting a business. Recent studies: Lussier & Pfeifer (2001)
6) Partners (part)	A business started by one person has a greater chance of failure than a firm started by more than one person. Recent studies: Lussier & Pfeifer (2001)
7) Parents (pent)	Business owners whose parents did not own a business have a greater chance of failure than owners whose parents did own a business. Recent studies: Lussier & Pfeifer (2001)
8) Minority (mior)	Business owners who are ethnic minorities have a greater chance of failure than non-minorities. Recent studies: Lussier & Pfeifer (2001)

9) Good Customer Relations (rela)	Businesses with not-so-good customers' relations have a higher chance of failure than those with good customer relations. Recent studies: Coy et al (2007); Chu, Benzing & McGee (2007); Benzing, Chu & Callanan (2005); Ghosh et al (2001); Voudouris et al (2000); Burns & Harrison (1996); Ghosh & Kwan (1996); Huck & McEwen (1991); DeHayes & Haeberle (1990); Ibrahim & Goodwin (1986)
10) Niches Market (Niche)	Businesses without a niche market will have a higher chance of failure than those with a niche market. Recent studies: Sum et al (2004); Ghosh et al (2001); Voudouris et al (2000) ; DeHayes & Haeberle (1990)
11) High Cost of Doing Business (cost)	Businesses with high costs of doing business have a higher chance of failure than those with lower costs of doing business. Recent studies: Camillo (2008); Gadenne (1998); Ghosh & Kwan (1996); Lau & Lim (1996)
12) Ability to Develop & Sustain technology edge (tech)	Businesses that have the ability to develop & sustain their technology edge will have a better chance of success than those without the ability. Recent studies: Ghosh (2001); Yeung & Chew (2001); Dutta & Evrard (1999); Cunningham (1995); DeHayes & Haeberle (1990); Bamberger (1989)
13) Competition (Compete)	Businesses with strong competition from competitors will have a higher chance of failure than those without/ less competition. Recent studies: Yoshi & Tuan (2009); Ghosh & Kwan (1996)

14) Significant 'People bonding' in firm (PeoBond)	Businesses with significant 'people bonding' will have a higher chance of success than those without 'people bonding'. Recent studies: Gadenne (1998); DeHayes & Haeberle (1990)
15) Access to broad Support & Resources (Broad Access)	Businesses with good access to a broad range of support and resources will have a higher chance of success than those without good access. Recent studies: Ghosh et al (2001)
16) Local Knowledge (LKnow)	Businesses with good local knowledge of the local business environment will have a higher chance of success than those without good local knowledge. Recent studies: Yeung & Chew (2001)

Table 14 shows the Personal Qualities Model which consists of 16 CSFs. An SME will have a better chance of success if: it has professional business advisors to guide it in the course of doing business; it has good working relationships between owner, staff and manager will have a better chance of success; it has good product and service timings whereby either very good old products or services or very good new ones; it has been setup during economic boom times; the business owner is not too young or too old; it has more business partners; it has business owners whose parents are also former or existing business people themselves; its business owners are not ethnic minorities; the business has good relationships with customers; it has a low cost of operation; it has good technological edges; it has less business competitors in the market; it has good intra-firm people bonding; it has broad access to a wide variety of resources; and it has good local domestic knowledge of the marketplace. The existence of all these conditions may have a positive impact on the profitability and thus success of an SME.

Table 15: Good Government Model (1 variable)

CSF/ Variable	Description & Recent Studies Done
1) Government Policy (govt)	Existence of good government policies will increase the chance of businesses succeeding than without good government policies. Recent studies: Neo & Chen (2007); Tambunan (2005); Hew (2004); Hogg, Medway & Warnaby (2003); Wagner, Fillis & Johansson (2003); Lawton (2002); Fischer & Reuber (2002); Ghosh et al (2001); Henderson & Robertson (2000); Mole (2000); Campos & Gonzalez (1999); Yusuf (1995)

Table 15 shows the Good Government Model which consists of 1 CSF. The existence of good government policy in general will help facilitate SMEs' business to succeed. Without good business policy in place, businesses will have a hard time trying to go about making their ends meet and succeed in the marketplace. Poor government policy in general will also result in more business uncertainty and poorer expectations for the future by SMEs and businesses in general.

Model 1, the (26 variables) Exploratory Model which this book is proposing, and Model 6, the control model (15 variables Lussier Model), are not shown here due to the large numbers of variables within each model. But these two models will be examined in greater detail in the subsequent chapters and the two models can be found in Appendix B.

More on the specific strategies and undertakings the Singaporean government has taken over the years and the relevance of these policies shall be discussed in the following chapter.

4.4 Sampling and Data Collection Procedures

The first main element of the methodology for this book consists of purposive sampling through contacting the business associations in Singapore, requesting their members to take part in the online web-based internet survey questionnaire. This is one of the most efficient methods to obtain information from specific target business groups.

Sampling through surveying of SMEs was initially planned by contacting the different business associations and chambers of commerce and industries in Singapore, requesting them to assist by mass dissemination of the survey information to their members (Galbraith etc al 2008, p. 188). An initial conventional mail was sent with a copy of the Invitation Letter, Information Sheet, Recruitment Material, and survey questionnaire addressed to the CEO or MD of the above mentioned business associations. One week later, the listed business associations' were telephoned in an attempt to speak to the CEO or MD.

However, this method proved to be unsuccessful as the respective business associations were either unable or unwilling to mass email their members, as they did not want it to appear to be an obligation for their members to respond to the research request. Instead, members had to be contacted directly through the internet listed business directories. Members of the SCCCI; SMCCI; & SICCI were contacted via email, one firm at a time.

The exact same set of questions was used for all the self-administered online survey questionnaires and the questionnaires sent to the participants who agreed to take part in the survey. The second main element of the methodology includes face-to-face interviews with senior staff of the government statutory boards to allow precise and accurate first hand information of the state of government SME policy in Singapore to be studied.

Following a modified version of Dillman's 'tailored design method', the survey measurement instrument (the questionnaire) was pre-tested twice before being sent out. First of all, the survey questionnaire was sent to PhD supervisor Professor Sajid Anwar and fellow office colleagues at the East Asian Institute, National University of Singapore for their comments and critique. Secondly, the survey questionnaire was then sent to a few friends in business and industry similarly for their comments and critique. In both cases, there were no particular criticism or comment and the online survey was deemed clear and usable.

The emailing of the questionnaires occurred in two separate waves. The first wave of individual emailing took place between 1 August 2009 and 30 September 2009. Businesses were emailed one-by-one as it was impossible to do mass emailing since the Internet Services Providers (ISPs) of many businesses prohibited such a practice. In addition, individual emailing s more personalized and potentially more effective. Between 1 October 2009 and 30 October 2009, all potential respondents in the first wave were sent a reminder email. A total of 342 businesses were emailed. As of 30 September 2009, a total of 44 completed responses were received, representing a response rate of 12.87 percent.

The second wave of emailing took place between 1 November 2009 and 30 November 2009. Between 1 December and 30 December 2009, all potential respondents in the second wave were sent a reminder email. This time, the potential respondents were also contacted by telephone and persuaded to take part in the online survey, by pitching to them the potential benefit for their businesses in the future. Some of the respondents in the second wave, whom initially said that they were not interested to participate in the online survey, eventually relented when told that they could do the survey right away on the telephone in just 5 minutes. A total of 469 businesses were emailed in the second wave. As of 17 January 2010, a total of 178 completed responses were received, representing a 37.95 percent response rate.

The survey questions seek to provide more detailed answers to the research questions/ hypotheses by probing the SMEs respondents as far as their companies' potential success or failure is concerned. The scoring/ points system which this book has adopted, allows the results of the questionnaires to be converted into quantitative data, which then enabled logistic regression and factor analyses to be conducted.

4.4.1 Identification of Research Respondents

The targeted research respondents were SMEs who are members or associates of the following:

- Association of Small & Medium Enterprises (ASME);
- Singapore Business Federation (SBF);
- Singapore Manufacturers' Federation (SMF);
- Singapore National Employers' Federation (SNEF);
- Singapore Chinese Chamber of Commerce and Industry (SCCCI);
- Singapore Indian Chamber of Commerce and Industry (SICCI);
- Singapore Malay Chamber of Commerce and Industry (SMCCI).

The internet web sites of the above mentioned and the business White Pages and Yellow Pages (both book and online versions) were also referred to as needed. In particular, the Singapore Chinese Chamber of Commerce & Industry (SCCCI) was targeted as it is one of the largest business associations in Singapore with over 4,700 members.

4.4.2 Type of sample

Purposive sampling in the form of judgment sampling targeting the proprietor or a top senior manager of the responding SME was used to obtain information from this specific target group. Several contacts in business associations in Singapore were able to assist in getting the initial invitation requesting participation to be sent out in the first place, which helped increase participation rates.

4.4.3 Sample size determination

A formula similar to (Cavana et al 2001) was used whereby:

$$N = \frac{[(k)(s)]^2}{E}$$

where:
N = sample size
K = z-score with a specified confidence level
S = sample standard deviation
E = error term or the level of precision in measuring the samples attribute

A sample size of larger than 30, smaller than 500, is considered to be appropriate for most research (Cavana et al 2001, p. 279).

4.4.4 Method of Contacting Respondents

A conventional mail containing the Invitation Letter, Information Sheet, Recruitment Material, and survey questionnaire was sent to the Association of Small & Medium Enterprises (ASME), the Singapore Business Federation (SBF), the Singapore Manufacturers' Federation (SMF), the Singapore National Employers' Federation (SNEF) and the various Chambers of Commerce & Industry; these organizations were also contacted by telephone to explain and to convince them to assist in this research study. SMEs who are listed members of these business and trade associations were contacted through their web listed email and phone contacts.

However, the total number of respondents who responded through the referral of the above mentioned business associations were low. At this point, listed members of the SCCCI were contacted directly by telephone, so as to make up the shortfall in the numbers of respondents, including those from the other business associations, whom did not reply. The SCCCI has a membership network of about 127 trade associations and 4,000 corporate entities including large financial and business organizations, multinational corporations, government-linked companies, small and medium enterprises from a wide spectrum of trades and industries.

Prior to the start of the online survey questionnaire and face-to-face interviews, the permission i.e. consent agreement of the owner/CEO/MD of the responding SMEs and the Singaporean government agency was sought in writing. For the face-to-face interviews, a short background brief of the subject matter was provided to the participating respondents, before the interviews took place.

Referral assistance (to contact potential respondents) and advice from Professor Wang Gungwu, a well-known person in Singapore, an internationally renowned scholar and historian, University Professor and Chairman of the East Asian Institute, National University of Singapore was also been sought. Prof Wang Gungwu is Chairman and an international advisory board member of numerous research, academic boards and journals in Singapore and overseas. He was formerly the Director of the East Asian Institute, NUS (1997-2007), former Vice-Chancellor of the University of Hong Kong (1985-1993), emeritus Professor of Far Eastern History in the Research School of Pacific Studies at the Australian National University (Professor since 1968). He was Director of the RSPACS (now RSPAS) from 1975-80; President of the Asian Studies Association of Australia from 1978-80; President of the Australian Academy of the Humanities from 1980-83; and award recipient of the Commander of the British Empire (in Australia) and Public Service Star (in Singapore).

4.4.5 Addressing Procedures for Sound Ethical Practices

No major ethical issue were encountered because all necessary information i.e. purpose of survey questionnaire; steps and procedures; company information; eventual research outcome etc are explained in writing and both surveyor and interviewees were asked to sign a consent & confidentiality agreement, prior to the start of the survey. Online respondents gave their consent by clicking on the online survey link. All information was strictly kept confidential and no names of persons or companies were identified. A one-page summary of the research results was to be made available to the responding participants if they expressed an interest in knowing the research outcome. So far, only one company has requested to receive this summary report. At any time, respondents could choose to opt out of the survey and their questionnaires will not be used, but no respondents opted out. All ethical procedures were considered throughout the entire research process (Tharenou et al 2007, pp. 216-226). The University of South Australia's Ethics Checklist was used to check for compliance and was submitted to the Ethics Committee for approval (Punch 2006, p. 57). Full approval was given on 31 July 2009.

4.5 Methods of Data Analysis

Self-administered online questionnaires were compiled and checked individually to ensure that they were completed and answered correctly. Only completed questionnaires were used. Incomplete questionnaires are not used; responses that had questions unanswered are not used (Cavana et al 2001, p. 316). The basic approach was to ask questions related to the independent variables in Tables 3 to 6. The statistical program SPSS was used to run two types of theoretical models (analyses) namely: logistic regression; and factor analysis to test and to measure the relationship between the variables in the theory (Tharenou et al 2007, p. 49).

4.5.1 Logistic Regression Model

Logistic modeling or regression was used to observe the relationship between the CSFs and a two-possible outcome: business success or failure. This model/ method is chosen because it can be used to predict a dependent variable (success or failure in this study) on the basis of continuous and/or categorical independent variables (CSFs) and to determine the percentage of variance in the dependent variable explained by the independent variables. It can also rank the relative importance of the independent variables; to assess the interaction effects; and to understand the impact of covariate control variables.

Equation 4a: Logistic function: $G(z) = exp(z)/[1 + exp(z)]$

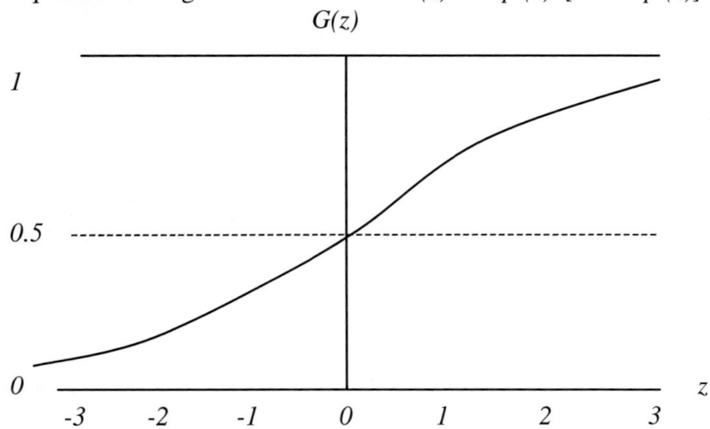

Graph 4a: Logistic function G (Z) = exp (z)/ [1 + exp (z)]
Source: Wooldridge 2000, p. 531

- *The logistic function, with z on the horizontal axis and f (z) on the vertical axis.*
- *Logistic regression is used here as:*

- a dichotomous outcome is needed (business success or failure)
- independent variables are of any type (age, strong leadership, resources etc)

Logistic regression predicts the log odds of the dependent (odds and odds ratios are explained further):

ln (odds(event)) = ln(prob(event)/prob(non event))

$$z = b_0 + b_1X_1 + b_2X_2 + ... + b_kX_k$$

where z is the log odds of the dependent variable and where b_0 is the constant and where there are 26 independent (X) variables, some of which may be interaction terms.

The "z" is the logit, also called the log odds. The "b" terms are the logistic regression coefficients, also called parameter estimates.

Exp (b) = the odds ratio for an independent variable

The odds ratio is the factor by which the independent increases or decreases. For increases in the log odds of the dependent, see discussion of interpreting b parameters below.

Exp (z) = the odds that the dependent equals the level of interest rather than the reference level. In binary logistic regression, this is usually the odds the dependent = 1 rather than 0. In multinomial logistic regression, this is usually the odds the dependent = the given level rather than the highest level.

Thus for a one-independent model, z would equal the constant, plus the b coefficient times the value of X_1, when predicting odds (event) for persons with a particular value of X_1, by default the value "1" for the binary case. If X_1 is a binary (0, 1) variable, then $z = X_0$ (that is, the constant) for the "0" group on X_1 and equals the constant plus the b coefficient for the "1" group. To convert the log odds (which is z, which is the logit) back into an odds ratio, the natural logarithmic base e is raised to the zth power: odds (event) = exp (z) = odds the binary dependent is 1 rather than 0. If X_1 is a continuous variable, then z equals the constant plus the b coefficient times the value of X_1.

For models with additional independent variables, z is the constant plus the cross products of the b coefficients time the values of the X (independent) variables. Exp (z) is the log odds of the dependent, or the estimate of odds (event).[51]

Binary (or binomial) logistic regression is a form of regression which is used when the dependent is a dichotomy and the independents are of any type. This book selected logistic regression modeling because the dependent variable is that of small businesses making a profit or not making a profit (i.e. profit = 1; not making a profit = 0) There are 26 independent variables / CSFs ranging from whether a small business thinks it has enough start-up capital to whether the small business thinks government policy benefitted them etc among others.

Unlike ordinary least square (OLS) regression, logistic regression does not assume linearity of relationship between the independent variables and the dependent variable, does not require normally distributed variables, does not assume homoscedasticity, and in general has less stringent requirements. It does, however, require that observations be independent and that the independent variables be linearly related to the logit of the dependent. The predictive success of the logistic regression can be assessed by looking at the classification table, showing correct and incorrect classifications of the dichotomous, ordinal, or polytomous dependent. Goodness-of-fit tests such as the likelihood ratio test are available as indicators of model appropriateness, as is the Wald statistic to test the significance of individual independent variables (Garson 2009).[52]

4.5.2 Factor Analysis using Principal Component Analysis

Factor analysis using principal component analysis is then used to reduce the number of variables from the original 26, to a smaller number of variables which helped to determine the main variables (CSFs) that contributed to firms' successes. Logistic regressions are run again to analyze the results of the reduced regression models.

Logistic regression modeling (Garson 2009; Tharenou et al 2007, pp.221-223, 230-231) and principal component analysis (Lussier 1995, 1999, 2001) are used to analyze the survey questionnaires to understand the attitudes of SME businesses toward questions relating to the CSFs (independent variables) (Seidman 2006, pp. 95-111). Logistic coefficients, also called unstandardized logistic regression coefficients, log odds-ratios, effect coefficients or in SPSS parameter estimates which is used in this study, correspond to *b* coefficients in ordinary least square (OLS) regression. Logistic scores are calculated whereby both logit (left-hand side of equation) and logit coefficients (right-hand side of equation) are being used for prediction purposes.

The second method of analysis, factor analysis, is used because it employs the technique of interdependency to find the latent factors that account for the patterns of collinearity among multiple metric variables, which this study involved.

The assumption that must be present for factor analysis to work is that:

a) There has to be a large enough sample to yield reliable estimates of the correlations among the variables;
b) The statistical inference is improved if the variables are multivariate normal;
c) The relationships among the pairs of variables are linear;
d) Outliers are absent among the cases; &
e) There is some degree of collinearity among the variables but not to an extreme degree or singularity among the variables.

The basic assumption hereon is that variables that significantly correlate with each other do so because they are measuring the same "thing". The purpose of performing factor analysis is to reduce multiple variables to a lesser number of underlying factors that are being measured by the variables.

There exist two main types of factor analysis. The first type is the "R" factor analysis which involves extracting latent factors from among the variables. The second type is the "Q" factor analysis which involves factoring the subjects vis-à-vis the variables; the result is a 'clustering' of the subjects into independent groups based upon factors extracted from the data. The "Q" method is not widely used today since a variety of clustering techniques have been developed that are designed specifically for the purpose of grouping multiple subjects into independent groups. This book uses the "R" factor analysis.

To summarize the above, factor analysis is a set of statistical methods which allows the reduction of a great number of specific variables and their relationships to a limited number of more general factors. A 'factor loading' represents the relationship (correlation) between a specific variable (item) and a more general factor (Bamberger 1989).

In accordance with what past researchers such as Danis et al (2010), Taylor (2005), Sadler-Smith et al (2003), Gadenne (1998) and Bamberger (1989) have done, factor analysis using principal component analysis was used to find the latent success variables or factors among the observed variables i.e. since data contains many variables, factor analysis can help reduce the number of variables and group variables with similar characteristics together. This book follows the above mentioned researchers in attempting to narrow down the initial long list of CSFs, to a shorter, more manageable list. The 26 independent variables in the main Exploratory Model (Model 1) and the rest of the reduced models are grouped into different themes and Principal Component Analysis is performed with Varimex rotation, to extract the main component factors. This is especially important for new survey questionnaires so as to explain multiple variables using a lesser number of factors. The following are the main actions & tests performed in Factor Analysis.

4.5.2.1 Kaiser-Meyer-Olkin (KMO) & Barlett's Test

Kaiser-Meyer-Olkin (KMO) & Barlett's Test. KMO measures sampling adequacy; if the KMO >0.5, it is alright for factor analysis to proceed. Barlett's test of sphericity (< 0.05 or closer to zero significance level) means the result of factor analysis is acceptable and the correlation matrix is not an identity matrix. If KMO & Barlett's tests are both acceptable, then the intercorrelation matrix is factorable; i.e. variables are collinear.

4.5.2.2 Extraction

An extraction method is performed using Principal Component Analysis. Component (Factor) matrix where loadings are >0.5 are being used. A rotated Component (Factor) matrix is used to reduce the number factors on which the variables under investigation have high loadings (correlations) i.e. making the interpretation of results easier.

4.5.2.3 Rotation

Types of rotation:

- Varimax: try to achieve loadings of ones & zeros in column of component matrix (1.0 & 0.0)
- Quartimax: try to achieve loadings of ones & zeros in rows of component matrix (1.0 & 0.0)
- Equimax: combines varimax & quartimax
- orthogonal: preserves the independence of the factors, geometrically they remain 90 degrees apart
- Oblique: will produce factors that are not independent, geometrically not 90 degrees apart

This book uses varimax rotation.

The Principal Components Analysis Method (Factor Analysis) is used because theoretically speaking, the variance of each variable is equal to 1.0. This study has 26 variables in total (for the Exploratory Model) and its total variance equals 26 which mean that its variance is too complicated to explain. The goal of factor analysis is to explain multiple variables using a lesser number of factors. A useful factor must account for more than 1.0 unit of variance or Eigenvalue ë > 1.0.

The analysis of the data occurred as soon as the online self-administered survey questionnaires and the physical copies of the questionnaires were completed. The web-based online surveys were automatically returned to the web hosting service and can be assessed for analysis almost instantaneously upon login. As the completed online survey questionnaires displayed no names whatsoever, it is impossible to know the identity of the respondents. As such, there is no issue about privacy as the online surveys are completely confidential. The only thing that appears on each of the completed online surveys is the internet protocol (IP) number, which is specific to a particular region or local area network (LAN) of computers. Only internet service providers (ISPs) i.e. the telecommunication companies will be able to know where the respective IP numbers are located.

4.6 Conclusion

Practically, Singapore makes for a good research location because the government of Singapore has been encouraging economic development mainly through targeted industrialization policies (on specific industries) and development of SMEs since the 1970s. The Singaporean economy grew and prospered mainly under the targeted industrial and SME policies which have been put in place specifically by the government, in addition to the CSFs firms identify from recent literature review.

Chapter five will discuss the results of whether SMEs in Singapore agree that good Singaporean government policies in general are beneficial, and whether the SMEs believe that there exists a list of CSFs vital for their businesses to succeed or which may cause their businesses to fail.

CHAPTER FIVE

ANALYSIS OF EMPIRICAL RESULTS

5.1 Introduction

This chapter discusses the results of whether SMEs in Singapore agree that good Singaporean government policies in general are beneficial, and if they believe that there exists a list of CSFs vital for their businesses to succeed or which may cause their businesses to fail.

Two types of analyses are being done. The first of which is logistic regression modeling which is followed by factor reduction analysis that is performed using principle component analysis. The purpose of performing factor analysis is to reduce multiple variables to a lesser number of underlying factors that are being measured by the variables. All the obtained results have Cronbach's Alpha values of over 0.7 and greater, signifying that the data are reliable.

5.2 Research Questions: A Recap

H1: Good government policy is an important CSF towards the success of SMEs;
H2: Successful SMEs have a list of CSFs which they can identify & adhere to;
H3: It is possible to forecast the potential success or failure of a firm using a prediction model.

5.3 Analyses of Results – A Brief Recap

5.3.1 Logistic Regression Modeling

This book use logistic regression and principal component analysis to analyze the results of the returned questionnaires (Tharenou et al 2007, pp. 252-259) and also identified, coded and categorized the primary data to see if there are any patterns (Cavana et al 2001, pp. 171); i.e. pattern of respondents either supporting or not supporting the hypotheses that their businesses have been successful or not as far as the various combinations of CSFs are concerned. As online survey questionnaires are used, the analysis of the research data is quantitative in nature.

Logistic coefficients, also called unstandardized logistic regression coefficients, log odds-ratios, effect coefficients or in SPSS parameter estimates, correspond to *b* coefficients in ordinary least square (OLS) regression. Logistic scores will be calculated whereby both logit (left-hand side of equation) and logit coefficients (right-hand side of equation) can be used for prediction purposes.

5.3.2 Factor Analysis

Factor analysis (reduction) using principle component analysis is being done as the third data analysis on the results, similar to what Danis et al (2010), Taylor (2005), Sadler-Smith et al (2003), Gadenne (1998) and Bamberger (1989) have done, as a confirmatory test to check the dimensionality, reliability and validity of all the variables/ factors.

5.4 Detailed Discussion of Results

As a brief recap, from August 2009 to January 2010, a total of 176 responses were returned or collected, from a total of 811 being sent out, indicating a total response rate of about 21.7 percent (176/811). Of these 176, only 146 valid useable survey questionnaires completed were from SMEs. The actual emailing of the questionnaires was done in two separate waves.

As mentioned earlier in Chapter 4, Questions 1 & 2, and 29-35 in the online survey questionnaire measured the fundamental conditions associated with the definitions of an SME business in Singapore, and attempted to also survey the type of industry (i.e. services, manufacturing, agriculture) the responding SMEs are engaged in, their company assets, average annual sales and percentage of sales meant for export.

5.4.1 SME Statistics

From Table 16 below, on Question 1 (regarding whether the firms were SMEs) and also on Question 7 (regarding whether the firms have assets less than S$15 million/US11.1 million), only 146 out of the 176 completed responses (83 percent) were SMEs. I.e. only those firms which answered (1), (2) or (3). As such only the responses of these 146 firms which are SMEs are used in the analysis.

Table 16: Summarized Descriptive Statistics of SMEs

Question	N	Minimum	Maximum	Mean	Std. Deviation
(1) **SME** (1: strongly agree; 7: strongly disagree)	146	1	3	1.72	0.692
(2) **Profit/Loss** (1: Loss; 2 & 3: made profit; 4: otherwise)	146	1	3	2.01	0.659
(3) **Which industry** (1: manufacturing; 2: services; 3: agriculture)	146	1	3	2.43	1.156
(4) **What products/ services** (1: FMCG; 2; consumer services; 3: industrial goods; 4: industrial services; 5: others)	146	1	5	2.69	1.342
(5) **Years in operation** (1: 1-3 yrs; 2: 4-6 yrs; 3: 7-9 yrs; 4: 10-15 yrs; 5: >15yrs)	146	1	5	3.40	1.506

(6) **Number of employees** (1: 1-10; 2: 11-50; 3: 51-100; 4: 101-200; 5:>200)	146	1	5	2.57	1.526
(7) **Total assets** (1: < S$1m; 2: S$1-5m; 3: S$5-10m; 4: S$10-15m)	146	1	4	2.29	1.528
(8) **Annual sales** (1: <S$1m; 2: S$1-3m; 3: S$3-5m; 4: S$5-10m; 5: >S$10m)	146	1	5	2.42	1.575
(9) **Percentage of sales for exports** (1:<5%; 2: 5-10%; 3: 10-30%; 4: 30-50%; 5: >50%)	146	1	5	2.30	1.573
Valid N (list wise)	146				

5.4.2 SME – Making Profit or Loss

On Question 2, the majority of firms (125 in total) that responded made profits (options 2 & 3). An additional assumption is being considered here; firms that answered either option (1) the 'loss making' option or (4) the 'otherwise' option were classified as loss making (i.e. option 1), since in the prevailing Singaporean business culture, some firms may be unwilling to admit that they were making a loss and preferred to select option (4).

5.4.3 Industry Types

Question 3 examined the type of industry the SMEs are engaged in. The vast majority of firms that responded are in the services industry (53.4 percent), followed by agricultural related services such as the importation of foodstuff, fresh fruits and vegetables (31.3 percent) etc (as Singapore practically has no real primary agriculture sector), and manufacturing (15.3 percent).

5.4.4 Product/ Service Types

Question 4 dealt with the type of products/ services firms provide. Most firms that responded are dealing in consumer services (55.7 percent) followed by FMCGs (10.2 percent). Industrial goods and industrial services both took up 5.1 percent each. The rest of the firms selected 'others.'

5.4.5 Years in Operation

Question 5 seeks to examine the number of years businesses have been in operation. 13.6 percent have been in operation for less than 3 years, slightly over a fifth have been in business for between 4-6 years; 8.5 percent have been in business for 7-9 years, about 16 percent have been operating for 10-15 years, and close to 40 percent have been in business for more than 15 years. In other words, over half of firms have been in operation for over 10 years, signifying these firms are experienced and must have somehow understood the CSFs of their respective businesses in order to have survived so long.

5.4.6 Firms' Manpower Size

Question 6 surveyed the sizes of firms. The majority of companies (32 percent) have less than 10 people; over half (57 percent) of companies surveyed have 50 people and below; a combined 17 percent of companies have between 51 to 200 people; & a quarter of companies have over 200 personnel.

5.4.7 Average total Assets of Firms

Question 7 surveyed the assets of firms. The majority of companies surveyed (41 percent) have less than S$1 million (US$740,000) in assets; over half of the total surveyed (64 percent) have assets below S$5 million (US$3.7 million); 19 percent have average assets between S$5-10m (US$3.7-7.4 million); just over 17 percent of businesses surveyed have more than S$15 million (US$11.1 million) in assets. Under the Singaporean definition of an SME, firms with greater than S$15m (US$11.1 million) in assets are considered non-SMEs and are dropped from this study.

5.4.8 Average Annual Sales

With reference to Question 8 in Table 16, the average annual sales values of the companies are surveyed. Most firms have less than S$1 million (US$740,000) in annual sales. Just over 57 percent of firms have under S$3 million (US$2.22 million) in annual sales, while just over 26 percent of businesses surveyed have more than S$10 million in (US$7.4 million) annual sales.

5.4.9 Percentage Sales meant for Export

In Question 9 of Table 16, the vast majority of companies surveyed (75.5 percent) have less than 5 percent of company's sales meant for export. Only 6.8 percent of companies surveyed have more than 50 percent of sales meant for exports, indicating that most firms are highly dependent on domestic sales within the Singaporean market. This is not peculiar as most businesses surveyed here are SMEs, and they have limited capability and capacity to export on a larger scale.

5.5 Results of Logistic Regression Modeling

With reference to the following discussion, the related Tables 18 to Table 30 can be found in Appendix B.

5.5.1 Model 1: Exploratory Model

The first model examined using the logistic regression technique is Model 1, which is the Exploratory Model with 26 independent variables. The complete model analyzed 146 of the 176 questionnaires and excluded 30 questionnaires from the study as a result of having at least one item with missing data or a 'not applicable' (e.g. non-SME) rating. The study results for the complete model containing all satisfaction items revealed a number of interesting findings. Within the complete logistic model, only the following four variables namely: Staff (p=0.074); Psti (p=0.043); Rela (p=0.065); & Lead (p=0.023) are significant at the 10 and 5 percent significance levels. This indicates that SMEs in Singapore view that having good high quality staff; having good new products/ services or older established products/ services; good relationship with customers; and having good top leadership among the senior management are very important CSFs for their business success. It is surprising that the 'Govt' (p=0.193) variable (good government policy) is statistically insignificant at the 10 percent level (but significant at the 20 percent level). As discussed in chapter two, numerous government policies exist for SMEs in Singapore to take advantage of, including funding opportunities.

However, a prevailing culture in Singapore is that businesses are often very passive, not proactive and take many things for granted. For example, many people regard the existence of a low crime rate, safe living environment and good legal institutions as a given. This may explain why SMEs surveyed in this book think that the existence of good government policies is statistically less significant. The exploratory model is also significant (p=0.045); see Table 18 in Appendix B. Table 17 below shows the list of the 26 variables and the associated descriptive statistics.

Table 17: Descriptive Statistics of Model 1- Exploratory Model

Independent Variables	Failed Mean	Failed S.D.	Success Mean	Success S.D.
(1) Capital (1 strongly agree - 7 strongly disagree)	3.25	1.511	3.01	1.532
(2) Record Keeping & financial control (1 strongly agree - 7 strongly disagree)	2.71	1.301	2.73	1.577
(3) Industry experience (1 strongly agree - 7 strongly disagree)	2.38	1.439	2.29	1.335
(4) Management experience (1 strongly agree - 7 strongly disagree)	2.75	1.567	2.58	1.521
(5) Planning (1 strongly agree - 7 strongly disagree)	3.29	1.628	2.82	1.448
(6) Professional Advice (1 strongly agree - 7 strongly disagree)	3.58	1.501	3.38	1.667
(7) Education (1 strongly agree - 7 strongly disagree)	3.08	1.792	3.08	1.728
(8) Staffing (1 strongly agree - 7 strongly disagree)	3.42	1.586	2.84	1.568

(9) Product/service timing (1 strongly agree - 7 strongly disagree)	3.75	1.511	2.89	1.425
(10) Economic timing (1 strongly agree - 7 strongly disagree)	3.17	1.786	3.20	1.639
(11) Age of owner (1: less than 20 year old; 2: 21-40 yo; 3: 41-60 yo; 4: above 60 yo)	3.50	1.615	2.96	1.543
(12) Partners (number of partners)	2.33	.868	2.30	.935
(13) Parents being business owners (1 strongly agree - 7 strongly disagree)	3.92	1.840	3.39	1.814
(14) Marketing (1 strongly agree - 7 strongly disagree)	4.54	1.641	3.66	1.848
(15) Minority (1 strongly agree - 7 strongly disagree)	3.83	1.926	4.01	2.015
(16) Relationship with customers (1 strongly agree - 7 strongly disagree)	4.17	2.239	3.48	2.062
(17) Niche product/service area (1 strongly agree - 7 strongly disagree)	2.79	1.318	2.71	1.229
(18) Cost of running business (1 strongly agree - 7 strongly disagree)	2.54	1.285	3.14	1.404
(19) Technology edge (1 strongly agree - 7 strongly disagree)	3.75	1.327	3.54	1.443
(20) Competition from rivals (1 strongly agree - 7 strongly disagree)	3.25	1.391	2.87	1.501
(21) Leadership of senior management (1 strongly agree - 7 strongly disagree)	3.17	1.523	2.45	1.163

(22) People bonding in firm (1 strongly agree - 7 strongly disagree)	2.67	1.239	2.62	1.025
(23) Organizational Capability (1 strongly agree - 7 strongly disagree)	3.42	1.283	2.91	1.207
(24) Broad access to resources (1 strongly agree - 7 strongly disagree)	3.21	1.318	3.08	1.366
(25) Local knowledge of market (1 strongly agree - 7 strongly disagree)	2.50	1.216	2.72	1.308
(26) Good government policy (1 strongly agree - 7 strongly disagree)	2.83	1.435	2.65	1.176

NB: The dependent variable was dichotomous i.e. business success (s=1) or failure (f=0).

With reference to Table 17, for example looking at independent variable 11 (Age of owner), the average age of an SME which fails has an owner who is between the ages of 41 to 60 years old (mean=3.50). On the other hand, a successful SME's owner is someone between 21-40 years old (mean=2.96). This suggests that, remarkably, younger entrepreneurs have a better chance of being successful than older entrepreneurs. This observation may be so because SMEs are usually nimble start-ups requiring a tremendous amount of time, energy and drive from its owners to make it succeed and younger people have more such energy and motivation to drive it.

5.5.2 Model 2: Good Management Model

Model 2 is the Good Management Model. At the 10 percent significance level, the reduced 8 variable model associated with 'Good Management' estimated that 'Plan' having a concrete business (Plan, p=0.097); having good marketing skills (Mrkt, p=0.099); and having good top leadership (Lead, p=0.058) are important CSFs for a firm to be successful. See Table 18 in Appendix B.

5.5.3 Model 3: Access to Finance Model

Model 3 examined the Access to Finance variable 'Capt'. At the 40 percent significance level (Capt, P=0.321), the reduced model on the explanatory variables associated with a firm's access to business finance, estimated that having sufficient initial business financing is an important CSFs for a firm to be successful. However, with a model significance level of p=0.327, Model 3 is insignificant at the 10 percent significance level. This result at first glance is surprising because it would have been thought that a firm's access to initial finance would be regarded as very important and thus being significant at a higher level of significance. However, recalling the findings of the Singaporean government from a study they have done previously as noted in Section 2.33, SMEs in Singapore list access to finance as not one of their most pressing success factors due to the existence of many sources of business finance available in the marketplace in Singapore. In short, Model 3 is not a good model. See Table 19 in Appendix B.

5.5.4 Model 4: Personal Qualities Model

Model 4 is the 16 variable Personal Qualities Model with a model significance of p=0.089. At the 10 percent significance level, the reduced model on the explanatory variables associated with personal qualities of the company estimated that having: (1) good staff (Staff, p=0.073); (2) good new or old product/ services (Psti, p=0.012); (3) parents who are also business people (Pent, p=0.040); (4) good customer relationships (Rela, p=0.085) are important CSFs for a firm to be successful. See Table 20 in Appendix B.

5.5.5 Model 5: Good Government Policy Model

Model 5 is the single variable Good Government Policy Model with a model significance of p=0.199. At the 20 percent significance level, the reduced log-log model on the explanatory variable associated with good government policy estimated that the variable 'Govt' is important for SMEs to be successful (p=0.193). See Table 21 in Appendix B.

5.5.6 Model 6: Lussier (1995) Model

Model 6, the Lussier (1995) 15 variables Model is used as a control model. The model has a -2 log-likelihood ratio of -57.657, which is the lowest (best) amongst all the above mentioned logistic regression models. The variables: having a business plan (Plan, p=0.071); having good new or older established product/ services (Psti, p=0.010); and having good marketing skills (Mrkt, p=0.027) are significant at the 10 percent significance level. See Table 22 in Appendix B.

5.5.7 Discussion & Results on the Comparison of Logistic Models

5.5.7.1 Logistic Model 1 vs Model 2

When Model 1 is compared to Model 2, there is a difference of about 63.83 in Bayesian Information Criterion (BIC') providing very strong support for Model 2 (the Good Management Model) i.e. statistically speaking, Model 2 is a better predictor as compared to Model 1, the Exploratory Model. However, the Exploratory Model has a higher classification accuracy compared to the Good Management Model.

The 26 variable Exploratory Model accurately predicted 86.3 percent of the sample as successful or failed businesses whereas the Good Management Model predicted 82.19 percent of the same. As 18 variables are decreased and subtracted from the Exploratory Model to form Model 2, it is expected that the ability of the model to predict will decrease. This is exactly what happened. If random guessing produces a 50 percent correct classification, then the Exploratory Model is 36.3 percent more reliable at classifying a specific small business firm as successful or failed and the Good Management Model is 32.19 percent more accurate.

On the ability of the variables in Models 1 & 2 to explain the variance in success or failure, the Cragg & Uhler's R-square is the same as the Nagelkerke R-square. It was used in this study and is considered to be similar to the R-square in regression. The Cragg & Uhler's R-square was 0.384 for the Exploratory Model and 0.144 for the Good Management Model, indicating a correlation between the predicted and observed group. This is reflective of the overall correct classification. In other words, 61.6 percent and 85.6 percent of the variance in success and failure of the Exploratory Model and Good Management Model respectively are explained by other variables that are not present in the models. By adding variables to the Good Management Model to form the Exploratory Model, it is expected and logical that the R-value of the latter would increase.

At the 10 percent significance level, the statistical outcome of the Exploratory Model suggests that: 1) having good high quality staff working in the company ('staff' variable, p=0.074); 2) having good product timings i.e. very new or old products/ services in the market ('psti' variable, p=0.043); 3) having good relationships with customers ('rela' variable, p=0.065); and 4) having good top management staff ('lead' variable, p=0.023) are vital critical success factors for small and medium-sized enterprises in Singapore. It is surprising that firms sampled in this study considered other factors such as the access to finance variable 'capt' and good government policy variable 'govt' as of lesser importance, as can be seen by their non-statistical significance (at 10 percent level) as compared to the above mentioned 4 statistically significant variables.

In addition, the Bayesian Information Criterion (BIC') shown in Table 18 in Appendix B, demonstrates that the Good Management Model, at 26.35 percent is a better model, compared to the Exploratory Model at 90.18 percent, which is surprising. However considering all the above factors, the Exploratory Model seem to be a better model as it captures a larger list of CSFs that SMEs ought to consider.

5.5.7.2 Logistic Model 1 vs Model 3

When Model 1 is compared to Model 3, the difference of about 86.15 in BIC' provides very strong support for Model 3 (Access to Finance Model) statistically speaking. However, the Exploratory Model has a better predictive ability, compared to the Access to Finance Model.

On the predictive ability (classification accuracy) of the Models 1 & 3, the 26 variable Exploratory Model accurately predicted 86.3 percent of the sample as successful or failed businesses whereas the Access to Finance Model predicted 81.5 percent of the same. As 25 variables are deducted from the Exploratory Model, it is expected that the ability of the Access to Finance Model to predict will decrease; the 81.5 percent prediction power shows this. If random guessing produces a 50 percent correct classification, then the Exploratory Model is 36.3 percent more reliable at classifying a specific small business firm as successful or failed and the Access to Finance Model is 31.5 percent more accurate.

On the ability of the variables in Models 1 & 3 to explain the variance in success or failure, the Cragg & Uhler's R-square (the same as the Nagelkerke R-square) was used in this study and is considered to be similar to the R-square in regression. The Cragg & Uhler's R-square was 0.384 for the Exploratory Model and 0.011 for the Access to Finance Model, indicating a weaker correlation between the predicted and observed group for the latter model. This is reflective of the overall correct classification. In other words, 61.6 percent and 98.9 percent of the variance in success and failure of the Exploratory Model and Access to Finance Model respectively are explained by other variables that are not present in the models. By reducing variables from the Exploratory Model to form the Access to Finance Model, it is expected and logical that the R-value of the latter would decrease.

In addition, though the Bayesian Information Criterion (BIC') shown in Table 19 in Appendix B, demonstrates that the Access to Finance Model, at 4 percent is a 'better model' (recalling that a lower BIC' is preferred) compared to the Exploratory Model at 90 percent, the model to be preferred is the Exploratory Model as it is difficult for a 1 variable model to accurately predict the success or failure of a firm.

5.5.7.3 Logistic Model 1 vs Model 4

When Model 1 is compared to Model 4, the difference of about 34.49 in BIC' provides very strong support for Model 4 (the Personal Qualities Model). However statistically speaking, Model 1 is a better model because the model significance level is p=0.045 whereas Model 4's model significance level is p=0.327. Model 1 also has a better predictive power compared to Model 4.

On the predictive ability or classification accuracy of the Models 1 & 4, the 26 variable Exploratory Model accurately predicted 86.3 percent of the sample as successful or failed businesses whereas the Personal Qualities Model predicted about 82.2 percent of the same. As variables are reduced, it is expected that the ability of the model to predict will decrease. If random guessing produces a 50 percent correct classification, then the Exploratory Model is 36.3 percent more reliable at classifying a specific small business firm as successful or failure prone and the Personal Qualities Model is 32.2 percent more accurate.

On the ability of the variables in Models 1 & 4 to explain the variance in success or failure, the Cragg & Uhler's R-square was 0.384 for Model 1 and 0.246 for Model 4, indicating a correlation between the predicted and observed group. This is reflective of the overall correct classification. In other words, 61.6 percent and 75.4 percent of the variance in success and failure of the Exploratory Model and Personal Qualities Model are explained by other variables that are not present in the models. By taking away 10 variables from Model 1 to form Model 4, it is expected and logical that the R-value of Model 4 would decrease.

In addition, the Bayesian Information Criterion (BIC') shown in Table 20 in Appendix B, demonstrates that Model 4, at about 55.7 percent is a better model, compared to Model 1 at 90 percent. Given any two estimated models, the model with the lower value of BIC' is the one to be preferred i.e. the 16 variable Personal Qualities Model may be preferred over the 26 variable Exploratory Model in this case. However, Model 1 with a more comprehensive list of CSFs provides a more accurate check-list for SMEs wanting to analyze their business strengths or weaknesses.

5.5.7.4 Logistic Model 1 vs Model 5

When Model 1 is compared to Model 5, the difference of about 86.85 in BIC' provides very strong support for Model 5 – the Good Government Policy Model. However, the Exploratory Model has better classification accuracy as compared to Model 5 (86 percent versus 81 percent).

On the predictive ability (classification accuracy) of Models 1 & 5, the 26 variable Model 1 accurately predicted 86.3 percent of the sample as successful or failed businesses whereas Model 5 predicted 81.5 percent of the same. As the number of variables is decreased from the Exploratory Model, it is expected that the ability of the model to predict will fall. If random guessing produces a 50 percent correct classification, then the Exploratory Model is 36.3 percent more reliable at classifying a specific small business firm as successful or failed and the Good Government Model is 31.5 percent more accurate.

On the ability of the variables in the models to explain the variance in success or failure, the Cragg & Uhler's R-square was 0.384 for the Exploratory Model and 0.018 for the Good Government Model, indicating a correlation between the predicted and observed group. This is reflective of the overall correct classification. In other words, 61.6 percent and 98.2 percent of the variance in success and failure of the Exploratory Model and Good Government Model are explained by other variables that are not present in the models. By subtracting 25 variables from Model 1 to form

Model 5, it is expected and logical that the R-value of Model 5 would decrease.

In addition, the Bayesian Information Criterion (BIC') shown in Table 21 in Appendix B, demonstrates that Model 1 at 90 percent, statistically speaking may not be a better model, compared to Model 5 at 3 percent. The BIC' of Model 1 increases as the number of variables increase. Given any two estimated models, usually the model with the lower value of BIC' is the one to be preferred. However in this case, the 26 variable Model 1 is preferred over Model 5 because it is not feasible for SMEs to depend on just 1 factor (i.e. good government policy) to predict if their businesses may be successful or not.

5.5.7.5 Logistic Model 1 vs Model 6

Model 6, the control model is tested using logistic regression to predict small businesses' success or failure. The results indicate significance of the Lussier model in predicting success or failure (p=0.057). For the coefficients of the model and the tests performed on it, see Table 21 in Appendix B. According to Lussier (2005) & Scherr (1989), the appropriate test for the overall significance of the model is the goodness of fit of the model, measured by the -2 log likelihood (LL) statistic. The LL compares the actual model to a 'perfect' model in which all cases would be correctly classified. In logistic regression, the chi-square for this statistic is used to test the significance level of the model, comparable to the F-test in standard regression (Lussier 2005, p. 50). As noted earlier and shown in Table 22, both Model 1 and Model 6 are significant (p=0.045 and p=0.057 respectively) for the chi-square statistic.

Difference of 39.91 in BIC' provides very strong support for Model 6 – the Lussier Model. On the predictive ability (classification accuracy) of Models 1 & 6, the former model accurately predicted 86.3 percent of the sample as successful or failed businesses whereas the latter model predicted 85.6 percent of the same. As 11 variables are increased and added to the original Model 6 to form Model 1, it is expected that the ability of the model to predict will increase. If random guessing produces a 50 percent correct classification, then Model 1 is 36.3 percent more reliable at classifying a specific small business firm as successful or failed and Model 6 is 35.6 percent more accurate.

On the ability of the variables in the Models to explain the variance in success or failure, the Cragg & Uhler's R-square was 0.384 for the Exploratory Model and 0.251 for the Lussier Model, indicating a correlation between the predicted and observed group. This is reflective of the overall correct classification. In other words, 61.6 percent and 74.9 percent of the variance in success and failure of the Exploratory Model and Lussier Model are explained by other variables that are not present in the models. By adding variables to the Lussier Model to form the Exploratory Model, it is expected and logical that the R-value of the latter would increase. From the above discussion, Model 1 seems to be a slightly better model compared to Model 6.

5.6 Discussion of the Exploratory Model on the Singaporean Context

At the 10 percent significance level, the statistical outcome of the Exploratory Model or Model 1 suggests that having: 1) having good high quality staff working in the company ('staff' variable, p=0.074); 2) having good product timings i.e. very new or old products in the market ('psti' variable, p=0.043); 3) having good relationships with customers ('rela' variable, p=0.065); & 4) having good top management staff ('lead' variable, p=0.023) are vital critical success factors for small and medium-sized enterprises in Singapore.

It is surprising that firms sampled in this study considered other factors such as the access to finance variable 'capt' and good government policy variable 'govt' as of lesser importance, as can be seen by their non-statistical significance as compared to the above mentioned four statistically significant variables at the 10% significance level.

In addition, the Bayesian Information Criterion (BIC') shown in Table 22 in Appendix B, demonstrates that the Lussier Model, at 50 percent is a better model, compared to the Exploratory Model at 90 percent. Given any two estimated models, the model with the lower value of BIC' may be the one to be preferred i.e. the 15 variable Lussier Model is preferred over the 26 variable Exploratory Model. However, the Exploratory Model, given its 26 variables, may be a better predictor for SMEs success or failure as the 26 variables can better capture a bigger range of CSFs. I.e. Model 1 is the preferred model to use in logistic regression modeling in this book.

5.7 Factor Analysis

The second of the two analysis methods used is Principal Component Analysis, a data reduction technique used to reduce the number of variables/ components/factors in a regression analysis (with many variables), into a more manageable/ reduced number of variables. A total of three data reduction exercises were performed namely for the full-model (with 26 variables); the good management-model (with 8 variables); and the personal qualities-model (with 16 variables) and Lussier Model (with 15 variables). Principal component analysis is not applied to the Capt (access to finance) and Govt (good government policy) variables, as these two variables are single variables in their respective regressions and cannot be simplified anymore. Only component matrices with a value close to or over 0.600 are considered.

5.7.1 Two main Types of Factor Analysis

There exist two main types of factor analysis. The first type is the "R" factor analysis which involves extracting latent factors from among the variables. The second type is the "Q" factor analysis which involves factoring the subjects vis-à-vis the variables. The result is a 'clustering' of the subjects into independent groups based upon factors extracted from the data. The "Q" method is not widely used today since a variety of clustering techniques have been developed that are designed specifically for the purpose of grouping multiple subjects into independent groups. This book uses the "R" factor analysis.

5.7.2 Factor Loadings

The component matrix indicates the correlations of each variable with each factor. For instance in the reduced Model 2, the total proportion of the variance in the 'Maex' (management experience) variable is explained by 0.659, or the sum of its squared factor loadings. This is called the communality of the variable 'Maex'. So in the reduced 'Good management-model' or Model 2, the original 8 variables are reduced into just 3 main groups of factors.

5.7.3 Data Reduction of Model 1- Exploratory Model

Table 23 in Appendix B shows the data reduction exercise using principal component analysis on Model 1 (the Exploratory Model with 26-

dependant variables). Model 1 yields a Kaiser-Meyer-Olkin (KMO) measure of sampling adequacy of 0.694 and a Barlett's Test of sphericity of 0.000, signifying that the results are statistically significant. Recall that KMO measures sampling adequacy, where a KMO value of greater than 0.5 is acceptable for factor analysis to proceed and a Barlett's test of sphericity of less than 0.05 or closer to zero significance level, means that the results of factor analysis is acceptable and the correlation matrix is not an identity matrix. There are 9 components/ variables with Eigenvalues of over 1.0. Among these nine component matrices, moderately significant component (aka Factor) 1 matrices are: Inex (0.603); Plan (0.618); Broadaccess (0.618); Govt (0.601). Moderately significant Factor 2 matrices are: Rkfc (0.637) & Rela (0.719). The remaining component matrices/ factors were of non-significance, as all components have component matrices of less than 0.6.

Rotation of Model 1 component matrix failed in achieving convergence (i.e. convergence = 0.000) in 25 iterations, signifying that the 26 variables are too diverse to be able to converge into smaller components.

Interpretation: According to Model 1:

1) *Relevant past industry experience; having a business plan; having broad access to resources; having good government policy;*
2) *Having good business record keeping and good customer relations*

Therefore, having these 6 CSFs are important for SME's business success.

5.7.4 Data Reduction of Model 2 - Good Management-model

Table 24 in Appendix B shows the data reduction exercise using principal component analysis on Model 2 (the good management-model with 8-dependant variables). Model 2 yields a slightly better KMO measure of sampling adequacy of 0.715 and a Barlett's Test of sphericity of 0.000, signifying that the results are statistically significant. Three components/ variables have Eigenvalues of over 1.0. Among these three component matrices, moderately good significant component 1 matrices are: Inex (0.755); Maex (0.801); Plan (0.726). The moderately good significant component 2 matrix is: Mrkt (0.796), and component 3 matrix is: Lead (0.639).

The significant rotated component matrices for Factor 1 are: Inex (0.842); Maex (0.764); Plan (0.727). Rotated Factor 2 matrices: Rkfc (0.769); Educ (0.595); Mrkt (0.613). Rotated Factor 3 matrices: Lead (0.819); Orgcap (0.636).

Interpretation: According to the reduced Model 2 having:

1) *Relevant past industry experience; relevant past management experience; a good business plan (i.e. Good relevant past experiences)*
2) *Good business record keeping; tertiary university education; past marketing experience (i.e. Good education and training)*
3) *Good leadership qualities and good organizational capabilities (i.e. Good leadership skills)*

Therefore, having good relevant past experiences; good education and training; and good leadership skills are 3 main groups of vital CSFs for SME's business success.

5.7.5 Data Reduction of Model 4 - Personal Qualities-model

Table 25 in Appendix B shows the data reduction exercise using principal component analysis of Model 4 (the personal qualities-model with 16-dependant variables). Model 4 yields a KMO measure of sampling adequacy of 0.630 and a Barlett's Test of sphericity of 0.000, signifying that the results are statistically significant. There are 6 components/ factors with Eigenvalues of over 1.0. Among these six factors, moderately significant factor 1 variables are: Niche (0.648); Peobond (0.654); Broadaccess (0.677); Lknow (0.598). Moderately significant factor 2 variables are: Pent (-0.630) & Rela (0.698); Compete (0.618). No factor 3 & 5 variables have a value of over 0.600; factor 4 variables are: Tech (0.740); factor 6 matrix: Part (0.804).

The significant rotated component matrices for factor 1 are: Peobond (0.724); Broadaccess (0.740); Lknow (0.718). Rotated factor 2 matrix: Pcti (0.744); Age (0.734). Rotated factor 3 matrices: Prad (0.609); Mior (0.605). Rotated component 4 matrix: Pent (0.638). Rotated component 5 matrix consists of the following variables: Tech (0.921); part (0.915).

Interpretation: According to the reduced Model 4, having:

1) *Good people bonding in the company; having broad access to resources; having good local business knowledge (i.e. being all-rounded)*
2) *Having good new or old products in the market; being of a certain mature age when starting the business (i.e. mature and with good products)*
3) *Having professional business advisors; being ethnic minority business person;(i.e. individual strengths)*
4) *Having parents whom were business people (i.e. business family)*
5) *Having a technological edge and having good business partners (i.e. being tech savvy with good partners)*

Therefore, having these 5 groups of CSFs are important for SMEs' business success.

5.7.6 Data Reduction of Model 6 – Lussier Model

Table 26 in Appendix B shows the factor reduction using Principle Component Analysis on Model 6. The KMO of Model 6 (with 15 variables) is 0.714 (good acceptability) and significant (p=0.000) and the rotated model produced 6 component matrices. Component 1 factors are 'Inex' (0.750), 'Maex' (0.787), 'Plan' (0.718) & 'Educ' (0.664); component 2 factors are 'Psti' (0.680) & 'Rfkc' (0.670) & 'Age' (0.721); component 3 factors are 'Capt' (0.601) & 'Ecti' (0.715); component 4 factor is 'Prad' (0.634); & component 5 factor is 'Mior' (0.812) & component 6 'Part' (0.819).

Interpretation: According to the reduced Model 6, having:

Relevant past industry and management experiences; having a good business plan and a good university education; having good new/ old products introduced into the marketplace; having good business and financial record keeping; being of a reasonable age (around 40 years old) when setting up the business; having sufficient initial start-up capital; setting up the business during an economic boom; having professional business advisers; being a non-minority and having good business partners are important CSFs for SMEs.

Therefore, being an all-rounded business person is a vital CSF for SME's business success.

From the above factor reduction discussions, it can be seen that Model 2 and Model 6 may be better predictors of CSFs among the four models as their respective KMO are 0.715 and 0.714, recalling that a KMO value of above 0.700 is good and any value below 0.700 is mediocre. All models passed the Bartlett's Test of Sphericity with significance levels of 0.000. However, this book believes that though the KMO of Model 1, the Exploratory Model is 0.694 (mediocre, but very close to 0.700), this model is still a valuable model because it consists of a much more comprehensive list of variables/CSFs (26 variables in fact) for SMEs to ponder about when running or setting up their businesses. Model 2 has only eight variables and Model 6, fifteen variables.

5.8 Additional Logistic Regression Performed onto the Models after Factor Reduction to Reduce Potential Multicollinearity

The following discussions link to Tables 27 to 30 in Appendix B.

5.8.1 New Exploratory Model – Model 7

Logistic regression of New Exploratory Model with 'logit' of profit/ loss as dependent variable, the average values of Component 1 matrices: Avg (Inex, Plan, Broadaccess, Govt) and the average values of Component 2: Avg (Rfkc, Rela) as independent variables was run. Model 7 was being run in accordance to the factor reduction results from the earlier subsection 5.7.3 (Data Reduction of Model 1), whereby Component 1 matrices (Inex, Plan, Broadaccess, Govt) and Component 2 matrices (Rfkc, Rela) are the remaining significant CSFs, after factor reduction. Logistic regression analysis of Model 7 reveals that the average of Component 1: Avg (Inex, Plan, Broadaccess, Govt) is statistically significant only at the 30 percent significance level (p=0.222) and that the average of Component 2: Avg (Rkfc, Rela) is statistically insignificant at the 30 percent significance level (p=0.438). The Classification Accuracy is 81.51%, -2LL is low (-68.85) and low BIC' of 7.861, signify that Model 7 is acceptable. These imply that the variables: Avg (Inex, Plan, Broadaccess, Govt) are important CSFs for small businesses i.e. relevant past industry experience, having a good business plan, having broad access to services and good government policy in general are important CSFs.

5.8.2 New Good Management Model- Model 8

Logistic regression of New Good Management Model with 'logit' of profit/ loss as dependent, the average values of Component 1: Avg (Inex, Maex, Plan) and average values of Component 2: Avg (Rkfc, Educ, Mrkt) and the average values of Component 3: Avg (Lead, Orgcap) as independent variables was run. Model 8 was being run in accordance to the factor reduction results from the earlier subsection 5.7.4 (Data Reduction of Model 2), whereby Component 1 matrices (Inex, Maex, Plan), Component 2 matrices (Rfkc, Educ, Mrkt) and Component 3 matrices (Lead, Orgcap) are the remaining significant CSFs, after factor reduction. Logistic regression analysis of Model 8 reveals that the average of Component 1 matrices is statistically insignificant at the 70 percent significance level (p=0.966) and that the average of Component 2 is statistically insignificant (p=0.720); only the average of Component 3 is statistically significant at the 5 percent significance level (p=0.021). The Classification Accuracy is also 81.51%, -2LL is low (-66.70) and BIC' of 8.546, signify that Model 8 is acceptable, though not as good as Model 7. These imply that the variables: Avg (Lead and Orgcap) are important CSFs for small businesses i.e. good top leadership and good organizational capabilities are important CSFs.

5.8.3 New Personal Qualities Model- Model 9

Logistic regression of New Personal Qualities Model with 'logit' of profit/ loss as dependent, the average values of Component 1: Avg (Peobond, Broadaccess, Lknow) and the average values of Component 2: Avg (Pcti, Age) and the average values of Component 3: Avg (Prad, Mior) and Component 4: 'Pent' and the average values of Component 5: Avg (Tech, Part) as independents was run. Model 9 was being run in accordance to the factor reduction results from the earlier subsection 5.7.5 (Data Reduction of Model 4), whereby Component 1 matrices (Peobond, Broadaccess, Lknow), Component 2 matrices (Psti, Age), Component 3 matrices (Prad, Mior), Component 4 matrix ‘Pent’ and Component 5 matrices (Tech, Part) are the remaining significant CSFs, after factor reduction. Logistic regression analysis of Model 9 reveals that the average of Component 1 (p=0.934); Component 3 (p=0.608); Component 5 (p=0.345) at the 10 percent significance level, are statistically insignificant. Only Component 2 (p=0.004) and Component 4 (p=0.050) are statistically significant at the 5 percent significance level. The Classification Accuracy is 80.82%, -2LL is low (-64.29) and the low BIC’ of 13.69, signify that

Model 9 is acceptable, though not as good as Model 8. These imply that the variables: Avg (Psti, Age) and (Pent) are important CSFs for small businesses i.e. having good products/ services and introducing them at the right time into the market; having parents whom were entrepreneurs are important CSFs.

5.8.4 New Lussier Model- Model 10

Logistic regression of New Lussier Model with 'logit' of profit/ loss as dependent, the average values of Component 1: Avg (Inex, Maex, Plan, Educ), the average values of Component 2: Avg (Psti, Rfkc, Age), the average values of Component 3: Avg (Capt, Ecti), Component 4: (Prad) and Component 5: (Mior) and Component 6: (Part) as independents was run. Model 10 was being run in accordance to the factor reduction results from the earlier subsection 5.7.6 (Data Reduction of Model 6), whereby Component 1 matrices (Inex, Maex, Plan, Educ), Component 2 matrices (Psti, Rfkc, Age), Component 3 matrices (Capt, Ecti), Component 4 matrix (Prad) and Component 5 matrix (Mior) and Component 6 matrix (Part) are the remaining significant CSFs, after factor reduction. Logistic regression analysis of Model 10 reveals that the average of all Component matrices, at the 10 percent significance levels, are statistically insignificant (i.e. Component 1 matrix, p=0.987; Component 2, p=0.112; Component 3, p=0.313, Component 4, p=0.848; Component 5, p=0.550; Component 6, p=0.507). The Classification Accuracy is also 80.82%, -2LL is low (-67.58) and BIC' of 25.26 is the highest among all four models (Models 7 to 10), signifying that Model 10 is least acceptable. These imply that the variables: Avg (Inex, Maex, Plan, Educ), Avg (Psti, Rfkc, Age), Avg (Capt, Ecti), (Prad) and (Part) are less important CSFs for small businesses.

On the whole, Model 7 (New Exploratory Model) seems to be the best model overall amongst all four models (Model 7 to 10), with the lowest -2LL, lowest BIC' and highest Classification Accuracy. Once again the Exploratory Model which this book proposes remains the most appropriate model of choice for business success/ failure prediction.

5.9 Implications and Conclusion

This chapter studied the effects of various critical success factors (CSFs) and management practices on the performance of small and medium-sized enterprises or SMEs across different industrial sectors, based on the Singaporean context. Two main methods of analysis: logistic regression and factor reduction were conducted in this chapter to examine which are the factors that are considered by small businesses, to be critically important for their businesses' profit/ loss performance.

Numerous research findings are worthwhile to reiterate in this study. Model 1, the Exploratory model with the logit link is the best model based on the screening criteria: the validity of model assumption, the fitting statistics (e.g., Person's chi-square and pseudo R-squares), the accuracy of the classification results, the principle of parsimony, and the stability of parameter estimation. Therefore, needless to say, major research findings and implications should be drawn from the best model.

Overall, this study should be viewed as an important first step for SMEs to explore the relationship between the overall business success and multiple explanatory variables concerning (a) government policy, (b) availability of business finance, (c) firms' personal qualities, and (d) individual firms' top leadership and management qualities etc, while pursuing their respective business activities.

The knowledge gained from this study will be beneficial to the business community in general, SMEs in particular; government bureaucrats; business academics and its students; and the interested general public. The goal is to obtain information from SMEs to establish benchmarks that could be helpful to decision makers in business, government and academia, for improving future business related policy formulation and research. For example, the business leaders could pursue its ultimate goal of ensuring business successes with better personal management and leadership training by, for example, taking more business management and leadership courses and personal development training. Government business policy makers could ensure that they continue to implement high quality, pro-business policies that support the business community in general and SMEs in particular, with relevant industry consultation and at the same time, working together with the employer associations and unions to achieve mutually agreeable industry and business outcomes.

In this study, the principle of parsimony along with various link functions has been adopted to build the candidate models and to search for the best model. Much of the time and energy has been devoted to developing candidate models, checking the model assumptions, assuring the model goodness of fit, and consequently selecting the best model. The various modeling techniques are actually practical tools that should be added to a practicing researcher's toolkit.

While the actual effects of the regression variables by and large confirm findings in the literature, some differences still exist between the results from the logistic regression models and the factor reduction models. This indicates that different regression or analysis models should be used with caution and their results accepted with a grain of salt.

5.10 Discussions of Government Policy

The two in-depth interviews with the Singaporean government agencies (Spring Singapore and International Enterprise Singapore) discussed in great detail, the programmes and government initiatives to assist SMEs grow and expand in Singapore, including the criteria for helping SMEs. The interviews revealed that since the early 1980s, the Singaporean government has undertaken a very systematic approach to assist SMEs grow and develop in Singapore and two main master plans have been developed for that purpose. The first SME master plan came out in 1989 and it was a detailed SME development road plan for the following decade from 1990 to 2000. A follow-up master plan called the SME 21 Master plan was subsequently developed in the year 2000 and in it are detailed plans to further develop small businesses in Singapore and help these SMEs grow beyond Singapore. The fact that such comprehensive assistance programmes are in placed suggest that good government policies are extremely useful and important for the growth of small businesses, and the evaluation of the relevant academic literature in this regard also confirms the importance of such pro-business policy for SMEs to be successful (i.e. *H1* is confirmed).

The empirical results of this chapter show that in Singapore, SMEs seem to adhere to the three hypotheses (*H1, H2 & H3*), that are important to the success (or failure) of their businesses. Furthermore, consciously or unconsciously, all SME owners have a list of CSFs at the back of their minds as to what need to be done or what conditions need to be present, for their businesses to be successful or otherwise (i.e. *H2* and *H3* are both confirmed).

However, this is not to suggest that the other CSF variables not mentioned in this book are unimportant; this study merely empirically analyzes which factors are deemed ‘more’ important than the others, as far as SMEs surveyed are concerned. In fact all factors are important and the list of 26 variables in Model 1 is non-exhaustive and there could be a lot more variables/ factors to consider, which can be the aim of future research.

5.11 Summary

It is convenient for some researchers to analyze ordinal outcome by means of logistic and linear regression analyses or the other way around, analyzing logistic outcome by means of ordinal or linear regression models. By altering the measuring scale of logistic or ordinal outcomes, researchers are able to analyze data and produce research findings and publications. However, the loss of information or incorrect analysis may have occurred in some cases. For instance, when the scale of outcome categories (e.g., making a big loss; making a loss; making a profit; and making a very big profit) is arbitrarily collapsed into a binary measure (e.g., making a loss and making a profit), researchers are forced to use logistic regression analysis to analyze the two levels of ordinal outcome. By doing so, important information may be lost in the resulting model.

Also, while few categories of ordinal outcome are treated as continuous measure, a linear regression method is used to analyze the ordinal outcome that cannot be plausibly assumed to have normality and constant variance. Using a linear regression method to analyze the ordinal outcome, researchers may produce incorrect estimations and interpretations based on the violation of the model's assumptions. Therefore, if researchers wish to study the effects of explanatory variables on all levels of the ordered categorical outcome, an ordinal regression method must be appropriately chosen in order to obtain the valid research results. In this study, the logistic regression and the factor reduction methods are used to model the relationship between the outcome variable, e.g., business successes or failures.

Essentially, sequential protocols are performed to create six different groups of models, all of which had profit/ loss as the dependent variable. First, all the 26 variables in the full Exploratory Model in this study are grouped to become Model 1. Second, the explanatory variables that examine good management styles are grouped under Model 2 - the Good Management Model with 8 variables. Third, the single explanatory variable that measure SMEs' access to finance is grouped as Model 3 - the Access to Finance Model. Fourth, the variables that examine SMEs' individual strengths are grouped as Model 4 - the Personal Qualities Model with 16 variables. Model 5 - the Good Government Policy Model has 1 variable. Finally, the last model with the original 15 variables from Lussier (1995) formed Model 6.

The logistic regression modeling method is the preferred research method and Model 1 is the preferred model and this book finds that four core CSFs must exist namely: having good staff (Staff); having good products that are either very new or established older products/ services (Psti); having good customer relationships (Rela); and having good top leadership in the company (Lead) are significantly associated with business success.

Factor reduction using principal component analysis on the preferred Model 1 yields six core CSFs namely: having relevant past industry experience (inex); having a good business plan (plan); having broad access to resources (broadaccess); having good government policy (govt); having good business record keeping (rfkc) and having good customer relations (rela) are significantly related with business success. A further logistic regression performed onto these six CSFs yielded the average of 'inex'; 'plan'; 'broadaccess'; & 'govt' to be statistically significant .i.e. more important when analysed as a grouped average.

5.12 Strengths

The strengths of the logistic regression and factor reduction models in this study can be seen from the above analyses. First, many indicators concerning business success and performance outcome are frequently of a binary nature measured on a logistic scale (i.e. win or lose; profit or loss). As earlier mentioned, unlike ordinary least square (OLS) regression, logistic regression does not assume linearity of relationship between the independent variables and the dependent variable; does not require normally distributed variables; does not assume homoscedasticity; and in general has less stringent requirements. It does, however, require that observations be independent and that the independent variables be linearly related to the logit of the dependent.

5.13 Weaknesses

Researchers need to be aware of the limitations in using any single model on its own. For instance, the "not applicable" responses of the survey questionnaire items (i.e. explanatory variables) are treated as missing values and excluded from the study. The large percentage of cells with missing data could lead to a decrease of actual sample size for the model construction or an inaccurate chi-square test for the model fitting.

Also worth noting is that the model goodness-of-fit is usually dependent of the chi-square test result. The chi-square test result normally depends on the sample size. Hence, if the number of cells with a zero value is large, the chi-squared goodness of fit statistics may not be appropriate. Thus, researchers are limited in how well they can assess the model goodness-of-fit. In addition, the logit link and cloglog link in the logistic and ordinal logistic regression analyses are not capable of selecting a subset of significant explanatory variables by means of automatic model building methods such as stepwise and back elimination procedures in SPSS command language. Therefore, researchers are obliged to rely on their own intuition and experiences to select a subset of the important or significant explanatory variables in the model. As a result, much of the time and energy is devoted to developing candidate models, checking the model assumptions, and assuring the model goodness-of-fit.

5.14 Major Alternatives

For other business performances rated on a grade scale, (e.g., win big, win, lose, and lose big) and satisfaction levels perceived by SMEs on a Likert scale, (e.g., very satisfied, satisfied, dissatisfied, and very dissatisfied), an ordinal logistic scale may be used instead. The ordinal logistic regression model is a variant form of logistic regression model.

The ordinal logistic regression method provides a viable alternative to analyze the success factors using data with the ordered categorical outcome. It does not treat an ordinal outcome as a binary or dichotomous measure like ordinary logistic regression analysis, which may lead to a potential loss of information. Also, it does not falsely assume continuous measure and does not require the properties of normality and constant variance (as for ordinary linear regressions to analyze few categories of ordinal outcome), which may lead to incorrect analysis. Clearly, the ordinal logistic regression modeling is a unique statistical technique in that the ordinal outcome variable is frequently encountered in the field of educational research and the model assumption of parallel lines is easily assumed and verified.

The ordinal logistic regression model is strictly built based on the model assumption of parallel lines (e.g., equal regression coefficients) for all corresponding outcome categories. If the verification of model assumption fails, the multinomial logistic regression model that does not require the model assumption should become an alternative tool. The multinomial logistic regression model is an extension of binary logistic regression.

In multinomial logistic regression, the outcome variable is categorized as the nominal groups--the target groups and the reference group. For example, 'good management' is labeled as group 1 success factors; 'access to finance' is labeled as group 2 success factor; 'good government policy' is considered as group 3 success factor; and 'personal qualities' is treated as the group 4 success factors. The 'full model' with 26 variables is the reference group. Three model equations are generated for the nominal outcome with the four categories. The three sets of relative risk are calculated when the probability of individual businesses falling into specific target category (j) is compared to those individuals being the reference category (k), e.g., P (Y=yj) / P (Y=yk) (Plank and Jordan, 1997). The magnitude of the effect of a specific explanatory variable can be expressed as an average of one unit change on an explanatory variable affects on the change of the relative risk of individual businesses falling back to the target category rather than advancing to the reference category.

CHAPTER SIX

CONCLUSION

6.1 Introduction

This book set out to explore the central themes on the importance of government policy and CSFs of small businesses, based on the Singaporean experience. The original contributions to knowledge of this book are namely: 1) an in-depth evaluation of government policy; 2) the identification of CSFs; and 3) the derivation of an exploratory model for the prediction of success or failure of businesses, particularly of SMEs, using empirical data from Singapore. Three major steps are taken to achieve the above mentioned in this book.

6.2 Summary of Research

Firstly, this book uses literature review to narrow down the CSFs of businesses, from businesses around the world, after which a list of the most frequently occurring CSFs are shortlisted.

Secondly, this book examines the broad theme of 'good government policy' and what has been done by the Singaporean government over time to help SMEs grow and prosper in Singapore. 'Good government policy' is also one of the main factors amongst the 26 CSFs, which are shortlisted from the extensive literature review on success factors for businesses.

Face-to-face interviews with the two main government business and trade promotion bodies, namely IE Singapore and Spring Singapore, are conducted to grasp the efforts of the Singapore government to help the SME sector develop and grow in Singapore.

Thirdly, this book followed on to examine the notion of business success/ failure, through the empirical study of CSFs among SMEs in Singapore via a 35-question self- complete online survey questionnaire. 178 responses are collected, while only 146 responses are deemed valid and suitable for use. Logistic regression modeling and factor reduction analysis using principal component analysis are applied to narrow down the 26 CSFs to a shorter summarized core list of CSFs, using the above two methods of analysis i.e. factors which SMEs in Singapore deemed to be more critical or important for their business success.

With the Exploratory Model (aka Model 1) as the preferred model, using logistic regression modeling, this book finds that statistically speaking: 1) having good quality staff; 2) having good products that are either very new or established older products/ services; 3) having good customer relationships; 4) having good top leadership are the top four most important CSFs associated with business success. Using factor reduction on Model 1, this book finds that: 1) having relevant past industry experience; 2) having a business plan; 3) having broad access to resources; 4) having good government policy; 5) having good business record keeping; and 6) having good customer relations are important CSFs for small businesses. A further narrowing down of the variables after factor reduction (into groups to reduce potential multicollinearity) revealed that group 1 with four factors: 'Inex'; 'Plan'; 'Broadaccess'; & 'Govt' are also important CSFs for business success.

A recap on the first Research Hypothesis of this book: Good government policy is an important CSF towards the success of SMEs. As discussed in Chapter 5, the empirical study of this book suggests that good government policy is indeed an important CSF that is very vital for business success. In fact, the good government policy variable 'Govt' is the most important CSF as compared to all the rest of the factors. H1 is thus positively verified.

The second Research Hypothesis is: Successful SMEs have a list of CSFs which they can identify and adhere to. As discussed in Chapter 5 under the 'Analysis of Results', it can be seen that a summarized list of CSFs (narrowed down from the initial 26 CSFs) is the outcome of the study. This signifies that a list of CSFs does indeed exist in the minds of most small business owners and managers, even if they (the business owners/ managers) may not be fully or consciously aware of the existence of such a list of CSFs. H2 is also affirmed.

The third and last Research Hypothesis: It is possible to forecast the potential success/failure of a firm using a prediction model. From the discussion in Chapter 5, the exploratory model proposed by this book accurately predicted 86.3 percent of the successful (or failed) SMEs whereas the original Lussier (1995) model predicted 85.6 percent. This is not to say that the control model (Lussier model) is not good (in fact both models are quite good), rather, that the Exploratory Model mentioned in this book may be slightly more suited to the Singaporean context. H3 is also hereby affirmed. SMEs can use the Exploratory Model that this book proposes as a checklist to gauge whether their overall business model is sound or otherwise.

This book helped establish benchmarks that could be helpful to decision makers for improving future business related policy formulation and research. Business leaders could pursue their goal of ensuring business successes with better personnel management and leadership training by for example, taking more business management and leadership courses and personal development. Government policy makers and others could utilize such a model to assess a firm's potential for success so that society could benefit via the allocation of limited resources toward higher-potential firms. The study introduces an exploratory business success versus failure prediction model, modeled after the Lussier (1995) prediction model, using data from Singapore. Using logistic regression analysis, it is found that the Lussier Model ($p = 0.057$) and the Exploratory Model ($p = 0.047$) are significant predictors of business success and failure.

6.3 Limitations

One major limitation of this book is that the research uses only one of many predictive models that are possible. There is a general lack of agreement among researchers worldwide as to what constitutes an exhaustive list of CSFs. As such, the proposed Exploratory Model 1 should only be used as a guide for businesses in general, both local and overseas. It is after all just a study and though great care has been taken to ensure that the 26 independent variables and their associated questions are relevant, businesses must not totally take the outcome of the results literally, as the list of CSF variables is non-exhaustive. There can never be 100 percent accuracy in any predictive model and such results have to be taken with a pinch of salt.

A second limitation of the research is that using Singapore as a case study may not be the most ideal. This is because Singapore is a highly regulated island nation that is only about 40 kilometers in length and 30 kilometers in breadth (maximum distance at both ends), 700 square kilometers in total land area, whereby the government has played and still is playing a major role in economic planning and development, and there are not many other countries that are of this situation or size in the world.

Last but not least, the usual limitations associated with cross-cultural studies also apply to this research; there are many differences between cultures which cannot be controlled. For example, there are differences in legal systems, economic conditions and attitudes towards business failure, propensity toward risk aversion and other factors (Lussier & Pfeifer 2001, p. 236).

6.3.1 Limitations to the establishment of Causality caused by Endogeneity

In any econometric model including the one used in this study, a parameter or variable is said to be endogenous when there is a correlation between the parameter or variable and the error term. An error term is a variable in a statistical model, which is created when the model does not fully represent the actual relationship between the independent variable(s) and the dependent variable. As a result of this incomplete relationship, the error term is the amount at which the equation may differ during empirical analysis. Endogeneity can arise as a result of measurement error, autoregression with autocorrelated errors, simultaneity, omitted variables, and sample selection errors. Broadly, a loop of causality or causation between the independent (CSFs) and dependent (success/ failure) variables of a model leads to endogeneity.

As far as this study is concerned, when predicting the potential success or failure of firms, for instance in the Good Management Model, the eight CSF variables 'Inex', 'Maex', 'Plan', 'Rfkc', 'Educ', 'Mrkt', 'lead' and 'Orgcap' are potentially endogenous because there may still be other factors which constitute good management practices, which are not factored into the equation or statistical model. In this case, there are limitations to the establishment of causality caused by potential endogeneity (i.e. businesses pursue entrepreneurial strategies in anticipation for their successful impact and do not usually bother if they perceive the opportunities for success to be limited). In contrast, a sudden change in for example, consumer tastes or preferences leading to reduced profitability due to falling demand for a particular business firm's products or services, would be due to exogeneity (or external factors).

6.4 Proposal for Future Research

There are many unanswered questions that are worth further researching. Why are there so many inconsistencies within the academic literature and that a single, universally agreed upon list of CSFs cannot exist? Almost all of the major variables identified as factors contributing to success or failure have been rejected by one or more other existing studies.

Since this is the first success versus failure prediction model based on the Singaporean context, the results of the model cannot be directly compared to other models. This Exploratory Prediction Model is based on a relatively small sample from Singapore. In support of the original Lussier Model, it should be stressed that the Lussier Model remains as useful and valid as before, as the model's original 15 variables form the main core factors of study in numerous other international studies around the world. It is suggested that the methodology used in this study be duplicated to conduct studies in other parts of the world, to see if similar or differing outcomes will result.

It is hoped that public policy makers and others could use the model to assess a firm's potential for success and society can benefit in direct or indirect ways via the reallocation of limited resources be it government aid, loans etc, towards higher-potential firms. However, it is important to note that predictive models are not meant to be a replacement for existing decision-making techniques. The Exploratory Prediction Model hereon does not provide numerical guidelines for variables distinguishing success from failure, and judgment is needed when applying it. The user must look at the list of variables in the model and subjectively assess the strengths of the business for each variable.

If a system of assigning a rating of strong, moderate or weak to each variable were to be employed, then an overall rating of strong, moderate or weak could be assigned to the probability of success. However, when the business is strong on some variables and weak on others, the assignment of a probability of success is a more subjective process.

The most promising finding of this research is that although there are great differences between countries, the Exploratory Model significantly predicts success and failure for firms in Singapore. Businesses in different countries may be more similar than is generally supposed and the model may be a significant predictor in other countries besides Singapore.

With the trend of increasing globalization, cross-national success prediction models will become more valuable. However, the Exploratory Prediction Model needs to be tested in other countries to further examine the predictive variables on a cross-national scale.

APPENDIX A

LIST OF ABBREVIATIONS AND ACRONYMS

ACE	Action Community for Entrepreneurship
AMP	Advanced Management Programme
ASEAN	Association of South East Asian Nations
ASME	Association of small-and-medium-sized enterprises
A*STAR	Singapore's Agency for Science, Technology & Research
B2BEC	Business-to-business Electronic Commerce
BAP	Business Advisers Programme
BAS	Business Angel Scheme
BERI	Business Environment Risk Intelligence
BLI	Business Leaders Initiative
BLP	Bridging Loan Programme
BUILD	Business Upgrading Initiatives for Long-term Development
CEO	Chief Executive Officer
CPF	Central Provident Fund
CSFs	Critical Success Factors
DTD	Double Tax Deduction
EBIS	Enterprise Business Information Service
EC	European Commission
EDC	Enterprise Development Centre
EDB	Economic Development Board of Singapore
EDS	Executive Development Scholarship
EF	Enterprise Fund
EII	Enterprise Investment Incentive Scheme
ESC	Economic Strategies Committee
FFP	Financial Facilitator Programme
FMCGs	Fast Moving Consumer Goods
FTA	Free Trade Agreement
GET-UP	Growing Enterprises with Technology Upgrade scheme
GNP	Gross National Product
HDB	Housing Development Board
HQ	Headquarters
IBF	International Business Fellowship

IDA	Infocomm (Information & Communication) Development Authority of Singapore
IDP	Incubator Development Programme
IFScheme	International Finance Scheme
IE Singapore	International Enterprise Singapore
IHL	Institute of Higher Learning
INSIS	Singapore Information Services Private Limited, a wholly-owned subsidiary of IE Singapore Holdings Private Limited
Ipartners	International Partners Programme
IPM	Intellectual Property Management
IRAS	Inland Revenue Authority of Singapore
ISES	Institute of Service Excellence, Singapore (under SMU)
ISO	International Standardization Organization
ITE	Institute of Technical Education
JTC	Jurong Town Corporation
KSFs	Key Success Factors
LEAD	Local Enterprise and Association Development Programme
LEFS	Local Enterprise Finance Scheme
LETAS	Local Enterprise Technical Assistance Scheme
LIS	Loan Insurance Scheme
MBA	Master of Business Administration (Degree)
MD	Managing Director
MDS	Management Development Scholarship
MIP	Market Immersion Programme
MNCs	Multinational Corporations
NPB	National Productivity Board
NTBFs	New Technology-based Firms
NTUC	National Trade Union Congress
NTU	Nanyang Technological University, Singapore
NUS	National University of Singapore
OBM	Original Brand Manufacture
ODM	Original Design Manufacture
OEM	Original Equipment Manufacture
OJT	On-the-job training
PEP	Pro-Enterprise Panel
PFI	Participating Financial Institution
PMET	Professional, Managers, Executives and Technicians
PSB	Singapore Productivity and Standards Board
SBF	Singapore Business Federation

SCCCI	Singapore Chinese Chamber of Commerce & Industry
SEEDS	Startup Enterprises Development Scheme
SICCI	Singapore Indian Chamber of Commerce & Industry
SISIR	Singapore Institute of Standards and Industrial Research
SMa	Singapore Manufacturers' Federation (formerly known as Singapore Manufacturers' Association)
SMCCI	Singapore Malay Chamber of Commerce & Industry
SMART	SME Management Action for Results Initiative
SMEs	Small-and-medium-sized enterprises
SMU	Singapore Management University
SNEF	Singapore National Employers' Federation
SP	Singapore Polytechnic
Spring	Spring Singapore
SPUR	Skills Programme for Upgrading & Resilience
STB	Singapore Tourism Board
SUPER	SME Upgrading for Performance
TAS	Training Assistance Scheme
TECS	Technology Enterprise Commercialization Scheme
TCIP	Trade Credit Insurance Programme
TCTP	Total Company Training Plan
TDB	Trade Development Board of Singapore
TECS	Technology Enterprise Commercialization Scheme
TIP	Technology Innovation Programme
WDA	Singapore Workforce Development Agency
WOG	Whole-of-Government
WSQ	Singapore Workforce Skills Qualification

APPENDIX B

TABLES AND FIGURES

Table 6: List of Participating Financial Institutions for EII

Participating Financial Institutions	Micro Loans	LEFS	IF Scheme	LIS	TCI
ABN AMRO			*		
DBS Bank	*	*	*	*	*
GE Commercial	*	*	*	*	
Hong Leong Finance	*	*	*	*	
IFS Capital	*	*	*		
Indian Bank	*	*			
Maybank	*	*	*	*	
Orix Leasing Singapore	*	*	*		
OCBC Bank	*	*	*		
RHB Bank	*	*			
Sing Investments & Finance	*	*			
Singapura Finance	*	*			
Standard Chartered Bank	*	*	*	*	*
HSBC Bank	*	*	*	*	
UOB Bank	*	*	*	*	

Source: Spring Singapore

Table 18: Logistic Regression Analysis Results of Model 1 versus Model 2

	Model 1: Exploratory Model		**Model 2: Good Management Model**	
Variables	**Coefficients β**	**Significance**	**Coefficients β**	**Significance**
(1) capt	-0.0735	0.757	-	-
(2) rkfc	-0.213	0.382	0.053	0.747
(3) inex	-0.176	0.563	0.000	0.998
(4) maex	0.179	0.477	0.184	0.379
(5) plan	-0.317	0.176	-0.296	0.097
(6) prad	-0.107	0.632	-	-
(7) educ	0.342	0.113	0.139	0.376
(8) staff	-0.34	0.074	-	-
(9) pcti	-0.432	0.043	-	-
(10) ecti	0.175	0.349	-	-
(11) age	-0.074	0.728	-	-
(12) part	0.057	0.864	-	-
(13) pent	-0.32	0.114	-	-
(14) mrkt	-0.253	0.189	-0.218	0.099
(15) mior	0.189	0.281	-	-

(16) rela	-0.341	0.065	-	-
(17) niche	-0.154	0.594	-	-
(18) cost	0.066	0.771	-	-
(19) tech	0.013	0.954	-	-
(20) compete	-0.062	0.776	-	-
(21) Lead	-0.611	0.023	-0.349	0.058
(22) peobond	0.271	0.452	-	-
(23) orgcap	-0.31	0.272	-0.208	0.312
(24) broadaccess	0.031	0.912	-	-
(25) Lknow	0.718	0.048	-	-
(26) govt	-0.352	0.191	-	-
Constant	8.77		3.85	

Model Test Results				
log likelihood	-50.21		-63.143	
Model chi-square	39.4		13.52	
Model Significance test	0.045		0.095	
Classification accuracy	86.30%		82.19%	
BIC'	90.18		26.35	
Cragg & Uhler's R square	0.384		0.144	
N= 146 profitable & not profitable firms				

Table 19: Logistic Regression Analysis Results of Model 1 versus Model 3

	Model 1: Exploratory Model		**Model 3: Access to Finance Model**	
Variables	**Coefficients β**	**Significance**	**Coefficients β**	**Significance**
(1) capt	-0.0735	0.757	-0.132	0.321
(2) rkfc	-0.213	0.382	-	-
(3) inex	-0.176	0.563	-	-
(4) maex	0.179	0.477	-	-
(5) plan	-0.317	0.176	-	-
(6) prad	-0.107	0.632	-	-
(7) educ	0.342	0.113	-	-
(8) staff	-0.34	0.074	-	-
(9) pcti	-0.432	0.043	-	-
(10) ecti	0.175	0.349	-	-
(11) age	-0.074	0.728	-	-
(12) part	0.057	0.864	-	-
(13) pent	-0.32	0.114	-	-
(14) mrkt	-0.253	0.189	-	-
(15) mior	0.189	0.281	-	-
(16) rela	-0.341	0.065	-	-
(17) niche	-0.154	0.594	-	-
(18) cost	0.066	0.771	-	-

(19) tech	0.013	0.954	-	-
(20) compete	-0.062	0.776	-	-
(21) Lead	-0.611	0.023	-	-
(22) peobond	0.271	0.452	-	-
(23) orgcap	-0.31	0.272	-	-
(24) broadaccess	0.031	0.912	-	-
(25) Lknow	0.718	0.048	-	-
(26) govt	-0.352	0.191	-	-
Constant	8.77		1.90	
Model Test Results				
log likelihood	-50.21		-69.42	
Model chi-square	39.4		0.96	
Model Significance test	0.045		0.327	
Classification accuracy	86.30%		81.51%	
BIC'	90.18		4.023	
Cragg & Uhler's R square	0.384		0.011	
N= 146 profitable & not profitable firms				

Table 20: Logistic Regression Analysis Results of Model 1 versus Model 4

	Model 1: Exploratory Model		Model 4:Personal Qualities Model	
Variables	Coefficients β	Significance	Coefficients β	Significance
(1) capt	-0.0735	0.757	-	-
(2) rkfc	-0.213	0.382	-	-
(3) inex	-0.176	0.563	-	-
(4) maex	0.179	0.477	-	-
(5) plan	-0.317	0.176	-	-
(6) prad	-0.107	0.632	-0.03	0.855
(7) educ	0.342	0.113	-	-
(8) staff	-0.34	0.074	-0.300	0.073
(9) pcti	-0.432	0.043	-0.482	0.012
(10) ecti	0.175	0.349	0.049	0.755
(11) age	-0.074	0.728	-0.059	0.739
(12) part	0.057	0.864	-0.176	0.513
(13) pent	-0.32	0.114	-0.352	0.040
(14) mrkt	-0.253	0.189	-	-
(15) mior	0.189	0.281	0.026	0.853

(16) rela	-0.341	0.065	-0.263	0.085
(17) niche	-0.154	0.594	0.082	0.729
(18) cost	0.066	0.771	0.272	0.201
(19) tech	0.013	0.954	-0.170	0.350
(20) compete	-0.062	0.776	-0.019	0.926
(21) Lead	-0.611	0.023	-	-
(22) peobond	0.271	0.452	-0.125	0.669
(23) orgcap	-0.31	0.272	-	-
(24) broadaccess	0.031	0.912	-0.104	0.665
(25) Lknow	0.718	0.048	0.449	0.98
(26) govt	-0.352	0.191	-	-
Constant	8.77		6.753	

Model Test Results				
log likelihood	-50.21		-57.88	
Model chi-square	39.4		24.04	
Model Significance test	0.045		0.089	
Classification accuracy	86.30%		82.19%	
BIC'	90.18		55.69	
Cragg & Uhler's R square	0.384		0.246	
N= 146 profitable & not profitable firms				

Table 21: Logistic Regression Analysis Results of Model 1 versus Model 5

	Model 1: Exploratory Model		Model 5: Good Government Model	
Variables	**Coefficients β**	**Significance**	**Coefficients β**	**Significance**
(1) capt	-0.0735	0.757	-	-
(2) rkfc	-0.213	0.382	-	-
(3) inex	-0.176	0.563	-	-
(4) maex	0.179	0.477	-	-
(5) plan	-0.317	0.176	-	-
(6) prad	-0.107	0.632	-	-
(7) educ	0.342	0.113	-	-
(8) staff	-0.34	0.074	-	-
(9) pcti	-0.432	0.043	-	-
(10) ecti	0.175	0.349	-	-
(11) age	-0.074	0.728	-	-
(12) part	0.057	0.864	-	-
(13) pent	-0.32	0.114	-	-
(14) mrkt	-0.253	0.189	-	-
(15) mior	0.189	0.281	-	-

(16) rela	-0.341	0.065	-	-
(17) niche	-0.154	0.594	-	-
(18) cost	0.066	0.771	-	-
(19) tech	0.013	0.954	-	-
(20) compete	-0.062	0.776	-	-
(21) Lead	-0.611	0.023	-	-
(22) peobond	0.271	0.452	-	-
(23) orgcap	-0.31	0.272	-	-
(24) broadaccess	0.031	0.912	-	-
(25) Lknow	0.718	0.048	-	-
(26) govt	-0.352	0.191	-0.209	0.193
Constant	8.77		2.073	

Model Test Results				
log likelihood	-50.21		-69.08	
Model chi-square	39.4		1.65	
Model Significance test	0.045		0.199	
Classification accuracy	86.30%		81.51%	
BIC'	90.18		3.33	
Cragg & Uhler's R square	0.384		0.018	
N= 146 profitable & not profitable firms				

Table 22: Logistic Regression Analysis Results of Model 1 versus Model 6

	Model 1: Exploratory Model		Model 6: Lussier Model	
Variables	Coefficients β	Significance	Coefficients β	Significance
(1) capt	-0.0735	0.757	-0.197	0.268
(2) rkfc	-0.213	0.382	0.069	0.721
(3) inex	-0.176	0.563	0.01	0.967
(4) maex	0.179	0.477	0.061	0.775
(5) plan	-0.317	0.176	-0.354	0.071
(6) prad	-0.107	0.632	0.055	0.762
(7) educ	0.342	0.113	0.162	0.373
(8) staff	-0.34	0.074	-0.156	0.299
(9) pcti	-0.432	0.043	-0.438	0.01
(10) ecti	0.175	0.349	0.116	0.466
(11) age	-0.074	0.728	-0.218	0.21
(12) part	0.057	0.864	-0.246	0.367
(13) pent	-0.32	0.114	-0.252	0.126
(14) mrkt	-0.253	0.189	-0.332	0.027
(15) mior	0.189	0.281	0.135	0.333

(16) rela	-0.341	0.065	-	-
(17) niche	-0.154	0.594	-	-
(18) cost	0.066	0.771	-	-
(19) tech	0.013	0.954	-	-
(20) compete	-0.062	0.776	-	-
(21) Lead	-0.611	0.023	-	-
(22) peobond	0.271	0.452	-	-
(23) orgcap	-0.31	0.272	-	-
(24) broadaccess	0.031	0.912	-	-
(25) Lknow	0.718	0.048	-	-
(26) govt	-0.352	0.191	-	-
Constant	8.77		6.753	

Model Test Results				
log likelihood	-50.21		-57.657	
Model chi-square	39.4		24.49	
Model Significance test	0.045		0.057	
Classification accuracy	86.30%		85.62%	
BIC'	90.18		50.26	
Cragg & Uhler's R square	0.384		0.251	
N= 146 profitable & not profitable firms				

Principle Component Analysis

Table 23: Analysis Results of Model 1

(a) KMO and Bartlett's Test

Kaiser-Meyer-Olkin Measure of Sampling Adequacy.		.694
Bartlett's Test of Sphericity	Approx. Chi-Square	1006.272
	Df	325
	Sig.	.000

(b) Communalities

	Initial	Extraction
Capt	1.000	.632
Rkfc	1.000	.675
Inex	1.000	.691
Maex	1.000	.706
Plan	1.000	.649
Prad	1.000	.569
Educ	1.000	.588
Staff	1.000	.322
Pcti	1.000	.705
Ecti	1.000	.592
Age	1.000	.663
Part	1.000	.701
Pent	1.000	.622
Mrkt	1.000	.700
Mior	1.000	.485
Rela	1.000	.702
Niche	1.000	.620
Cost	1.000	.654
Tech	1.000	.830
Compete	1.000	.753
Lead	1.000	.758
Peobond	1.000	.569
Orgcap	1.000	.503
Broadaccess	1.000	.677
Lknow	1.000	.738
Govt	1.000	.642

Extraction Method: Principal Component Analysis.

(c) Component Matrix[a]
Component

	1	2	3	4	5	6	7	8	9
Capt	.183	-.556	-.091	-.037	.462	.141	-.195		-.076
Rkfc	.240	.637	-.174	-.200	-.041	.010	.106	-.303	-.194
Inex	.603	-.053	-.487	-.160	-.178	-.109	-.036	.020	-.127
Maex	.537	.042	-.561	.174	-.214	.031	-.090	.037	.121
Plan	.618	-.043	-.462	.095	.131	-.085	-.096	.086	.041
Prad	.582	-.058	-.192	-.149	.270	.015	.273	.107	.096
Educ	.401	.346	-.363	.050	-.185	-.098	.227	.277	.031
Staff	.440	-.125	-.031	-.030	-.052	.156	-.230	-.096	-.147
Pcti	.289	.352	.242	-.405	.136	.392	-.126	-.120	.269
Ecti	.357	-.230	-.033	-.305	.215	.435	-.072	.163	-.224
Age	-.034	.549	-.101	-.239	.110	.447	-.022	.164	.232
Part	.131	-.174	.076	-.118	-.477	.276	.440	-.239	.283
Pent	.164	-.580	.005	.220	-.130	-.058	.000	.195	.391
Mrkt	.030	.422	.043	.499	.446	-.055	.214	.007	.148
Mior	.293	-.450	.232	.034	.165	.009	.331	.004	.072
Rela	-.005	.719	.119	.178	.063	-.019	.269	.248	-.034
Niche	.522	-.046	.374	-.213	.011	.057	.267	.160	-.244
Cost	.287	-.160	.356	-.196	-.498	-.127	-.125	.310	-.072
Tech	.116	.048	.196	.488	-.126	.424	-.036	.473	-.342
Compete	.085	.520	.182	-.046	-.079	-.067	-.493	.209	.378
Lead	.297	-.043	.037	.564	-.109	.454	-.036	-.358	.044
Peobond	.561	.099	.363	.152	-.100	-.145	-.190	-.142	.052
Orgcap	.584	.005	.130	.230	-.117	.103	-.168	-.199	.025
Broadaccess	.618	.046	.255	.030	.320	-.302	-.184	.005	-.005
Lknow	.551	.406	.238	.013	-.081	-.228	.064	-.274	-.274
Govt	.601	-.174	.257	-.076	.132	-.139	.215	.086	.297

Extraction Method: Principal Component Analysis.
a. 9 components extracted.

Table 24: Analysis Results of Model 2
(a) KMO and Bartlett's Test

Kaiser-Meyer-Olkin Measure of Sampling Adequacy.		.715
Bartlett's Test of Sphericity	Approx. Chi-Square	199.825
	df	28
	Sig.	.000

(b) Communalities

	Initial	Extraction
Rkfc	1.000	.621
Inex	1.000	.710
Maex	1.000	.659
Plan	1.000	.560
Educ	1.000	.575
Lead	1.000	.674
Mrkt	1.000	.638
Orgcap	1.000	.568

Extraction Method: Principal Component Analysis.

(c) Rotated Component Matrix[a]

Component

	1	2	3
Rkfc	.156	.769	-.079
Inex	.842	.040	-.015
Maex	.764	.140	.237
Plan	.727	.093	.154
Educ	.463	.595	-.079
Lead	.048	.031	.819
Mrkt	-.301	.613	.415
Orgcap	.398	-.073	.636

Extraction Method: Principal Component Analysis.
Rotation Method: Varimax with Kaiser Normalization.
a. Rotation converged in 7 iterations.

Table 25: Analysis Results of Model 4

(a) KMO and Bartlett's Test

Kaiser-Meyer-Olkin Measure of Sampling Adequacy.		.630
Bartlett's Test of Sphericity	Approx. Chi-Square	386.974
	df	120
	Sig.	.000

(b) Communalities

	Initial	Extraction
Prad	1.000	.505
Staff	1.000	.464
Pcti	1.000	.647
Ecti	1.000	.595
Age	1.000	.609
Part	1.000	.855
Pent	1.000	.539
Mior	1.000	.479
Rela	1.000	.631
Niche	1.000	.604
Cost	1.000	.554
Tech	1.000	.854
Compete	1.000	.607
Peobond	1.000	.562
Broadaccess	1.000	.674
Lknow	1.000	.533

Extraction Method: Principal Component Analysis.

(c) Rotated Component Matrix[a]
Component

	1	2	3	4	5	6
Prad	.303	.171	.609	.001	-.115	.014
Staff	.208	.229	.121	.588	.004	-.086
Pcti	.231	.744	.079	.050	-.117	.134
Ecti	-.092	.373	.537	.336	.176	-.127
Age	-.126	.734	-.085	-.192	.080	-.056
Part	-.052	.025	.083	.068	-.048	.915
Pent	-.110	-.319	.114	.638	-.017	.068
Mior	.112	-.247	.605	.190	-.011	.049
Rela	.253	.302	-.260	-.527	.362	.015
Niche	.457	.082	.489	-.038	.252	.290
Cost	.313	-.048	-.102	.577	.227	.241
Tech	.021	-.033	.030	.048	.921	-.041
Compete	.368	.405	-.540	.022	.012	-.125
Peobond	.724	-.014	.034	.164	.039	.086
Broadaccess	.740	-.027	.266	.025	-.078	-.220
Lknow	.718	.119	-.004	-.026	.057	.004

Extraction Method: Principal Component Analysis.
Rotation Method: Varimax with Kaiser Normalization.
a. Rotation converged in 8 iterations.

Table 26: Analysis Results of Model 6
(a) KMO and Bartlett's Test

Kaiser-Meyer-Olkin Measure of Sampling Adequacy.		.714
Bartlett's Test of Sphericity	Approx. Chi-Square	390.642
	df	105
	Sig.	.000

(b) Communalities

	Initial	Extraction
Capt	1.000	.554
Rkfc	1.000	.584
Inex	1.000	.642
Maex	1.000	.627
Plan	1.000	.633
Prad	1.000	.659
Educ	1.000	.519
Staff	1.000	.367
Pcti	1.000	.635
Ecti	1.000	.549
Age	1.000	.528
Part	1.000	.743
Pent	1.000	.448
Mrkt	1.000	.637
Mior	1.000	.722

Extraction Method: Principal Component Analysis.

(c) Rotated Component Matrix[a]

Component

	1	2	3	4	5
Capt	-.050	-.351	.601	.208	-.153
Rkfc	.324	.670	-.137	-.065	-.076
Inex	.750	-.042	.236	.028	.145
Maex	.787	-.031	.046	.063	.029
Plan	.718	-.061	.289	.130	-.116
Prad	.435	.158	.200	.634	-.054
Educ	.664	.209	-.178	-.050	-.013
Staff	.266	.006	.543	-.024	.025
Pcti	-.071	.680	.351	.156	.142
Ecti	.067	.101	.715	.117	.097
Age	-.007	.721	-.034	-.001	-.083
Part	.061	.016	-.150	.216	.819
Pent	.094	-.572	.111	.296	.111
Mrkt	.033	.204	-.307	.251	-.661
Mior	-.067	-.217	.084	.812	.068

Extraction Method: Principal Component Analysis.
Rotation Method: Varimax with Kaiser Normalization.
a. Rotation converged in 6 iterations.

Table 27: Logistic Regression Results of New Exploratory Model 7

	New Exploratory Model 7	
Variables	**Coefficients β**	**Significance**
Component 1: Avg(Inex, Plan, Broadaccess, Govt)	0.259	0.222
Component 2: Avg(Rfkc, Rela)	0.116	0.438
Constant	-2.591	0.001
Model Test Results		
log likelihood	-68.85	
Model chi-square	2.11	
Model Significance test	0.348	
Classification accuracy	81.51%	
BIC'	7.861	
Cragg & Uhler's R square	0.023	
N= 146 profitable & not profitable firms		

Table 28: Logistic Regression Results of New Good Management Model 8

	New Good Management Model 8	
Variables	**Coefficients β**	**Significance**
Component 1: Avg(Inex, Maex, Plan)	-0.008	0.966
Component 2: Avg(Rfkc, Educ, Mrkt)	0.072	0.720
Component 3: Avg(Lead, Orgcap)	0.515	0.021
Constant	-3.211	0.000
Model Test Results		
log likelihood	-66.70	
Model chi-square	6.40	
Model Significance test	0.093	
Classification accuracy	81.51%	
BIC'	8.546	
Cragg & Uhler's R square	0.070	
N= 146 profitable & not profitable firms		

Table 29: Logistic Regression Results of New Personal Qualities Model 9

	New Personal Qualities Model 9	
Variables	**Coefficients β**	**Significance**
Component 1: Avg(Peobond, Broadaccess, Lknow)	-0.019	0.934
Component 2: Avg(Pcti, Age)	0.559	0.004
Component 3: Avg(Prad, Mior)	-0.085	0.608
Component 4: Pent	0.273	0.050
Component 5: Avg(Tech, Part)	0.262	0.345
Constant	-4.719	0.002
Model Test Results		
log likelihood	-64.29	
Model chi-square	11.22	
Model Significance test	0.047	
Classification accuracy	80.82%	
BIC'	13.69	
Cragg & Uhler's R square	0.12	
N= 146 profitable & not profitable firms		

Table 30: Logistic Regression Results of New Lussier Model 10

	New Lussier Model 10	
Variables	**Coefficients β**	**Significance**
Component 1: Avg(Inex, Maex, Plan, Educ)	0.003	0.987
Component 2: Avg(Psti, Rfkc, Age)	0.310	0.112
Component 3: Avg(Capt, Ecti)	0.178	0.313
Component 4: Prad	0.030	0.848
Component 5: Mior	-0.072	0.550
Component 6: Part	0.156	0.507
Constant	-3.21	0.008
Model Test Results		
log likelihood	-67.58	
Model chi-square	4.647	
Model Significance test	0.591	
Classification accuracy	80.82%	
BIC'	25.26	
Cragg & Uhler's R square	0.051	
N= 146 profitable & not profitable firms		

APPENDIX C

SME 21 (2000) STRATEGIES

SME 21 lst-Prong Strategies: Enterprise-level Strategies and SME Development Programmes

Strategies	Programmes
1) Developing Entrepreneurs and Employees	- SME Mentoring Programme to help SMEs map out strategic directions - SME Circles (EntreNet) to provide SMEs with learning partners - Entrepreneurship Education to equip entrepreneurs with management and leadership skills - SME Virtual University to provide IT and e-business courses to SMEs through the internet
2) Managing Business Excellence	- Business Excellence Framework to help SMEs manage their organizations professionally - National Best Practice Center to help SME learn from and apply best practices - A pool of professional managers to help transform SMEs into professionally-run organizations - Assistance for SMEs to set-up effective value and cost management systems

3) Harnessing Technology and Knowledge for Growth	- SME Business Support Centers to offer a wide array of integrated business support services and advice to SMEs - Technology Network (TechNet) Programme to facilitate connections between aspiring technopreneurs, innovative SMEs, researchers and experts and venture capitalists - Technology Incubator Programme to provide SMEs with access to management assistance, finance and business and technical support services
4) Designing New Business Models for Competitive Advantage	- Strategic Business Planning self-help package to enable SMEs to develop their own strategic business plans - Innovative Business Concept Award to spur SMEs to continuously develop new business concepts

Source: SME 21

SME 21 2nd-Prong Strategies: Sector-level Strategies and SME Development Programmes

Strategies	Programmes
1)Facilitating Collaborative Partnerships and Strategic Alliances	- Franchising and economic groupings as strategic tools to help domestic businesses become regional and global players - Shared services to help SMEs better manage their costs and resources, and focus on core activities - Business fusion groups for SMEs to continuously develop new business concepts
2)Upgrading Domestic Service Sectors	- Industry Upgrading Programme to raise the productivity of tradable and non-tradable sectors - Upgrading assistance programmes to help domestic businesses overcome the disadvantage of size, build up capabilities to grow, leverage on the internet to do business and be internationally competitive - A comprehensive range of measures to restructure, revitalize and upgrade the retail sector - A wide range of programmes to upgrade the construction sector

Source: SME 21

SME 21 3rd-Prong Strategies: Broad-based Strategies and SME Development Programmes

Strategies	Programmes
1)Promoting Entrepreneurship	-A 'SME March' with month-long activities to convey the message that SMEs need to forge ahead and change their mindset -Media programmes to raise the profile of SMEs in Singapore -Local SMEs promoted as preferred business partners to foreign companies
2)Financing for Growth	- Business Angel Network to promote equity financing for innovative and high growth firms - Business-to-business (B2B) working capital matching service to help SMEs in need of working capital to purchase raw material or to fulfill a contract - SME schemes reviewed constantly to ensure their relevance and effectiveness in Singapore's knowledge-based economy -Economic value-added promoted as a tool for measuring the effectiveness of capital usage
3)Facilitating Market Access	- BusinessConnect Programme more widely promoted and enhanced - SingaporeConnect publicized widely to more SMEs; linkages with databases of other countries, as well as local and foreign industry associations and chambers accelerated - Importance of branding promoted to SMEs; unique Singapore brand image developed for SMEs to leverage on as they explore new markets overseas

4)Strengthening Local Talent	- More SME scholarships developed to groom local talent - Effective systems put in place to facilitate lifelong learning and skills development in organizations - Foreign talent tapped through various measures and programmes
5)Accelerating E-commerce	- Promising e-commerce SMEs identifies and developed as role models - Adoption of B2B portals by SMEs encouraged and accelerated - One-stop SME portal for foreign and local SMES created to access the required information and services easily - E-commerce infrastructure in Singapore developed
6)Promoting Singapore as an SME Hub	- Economic twinning programmes with other countries identified and pursued to establish areas for SME collaboration - Concerted marketing effort to encourage SMEs to use Singapore as the conduit and venue for international transactions - Chambers of commerce and industry associations as information and networking platform providers for foreign SMEs to meet up with their local counterparts - A package of fiscal measures to attract foreign SMEs to locate in Singapore - SME community created to attract foreign SMEs to start their operations here - Financing for collaborations between foreign and local SMEs to take place

Source: SME 21

APPENDIX D

COPY OF RESEARCH SURVEY QUESTIONNAIRE (SMEs)

1. Is your company a small and medium-sized enterprise (SME)? funds and not facing initial financial difficulty)?

1) Strongly Agree
2) Agree
3) Somewhat Agree
4) Neutral/ Can't Tell
5) Somewhat Disagree
6) Disagree
7) Strongly Disagree

2. Did your company in the last 3 years

1) Lose Money
2) Make Industry Average Profit
3) Greater Profits
4) Otherwise

3. Is your company well capitalized when initially started (has sufficient start-up

1) Strongly Agree
2) Agree
3) Somewhat Agree
4) Neutral/ Can't Tell
5) Somewhat Disagree
6) Disagree
7) Strongly Disagree

4. Is your company keeping updated and accurate financial records?

1) Strongly Agree
2) Agree
3) Somewhat Agree
4) Neutral/ Can't Tell
5) Somewhat Disagree
6) Disagree
7) Strongly Disagree

5. Is your company managed by people with prior industry experience?

1) Strongly Agree
2) Agree
3) Somewhat Agree
4) Neutral/ Can't Tell
5) Somewhat Disagree
6) Disagree
7) Strongly Disagree

6. Is your company managed by people with prior management experience?

1) Strongly Agree
2) Agree
3) Somewhat Agree
4) Neutral/ Can't Tell
5) Somewhat Disagree
6) Disagree
7) Strongly Disagree

7. Is your company operating using a specific business plan?

1) Strongly Agree
2) Agree
3) Somewhat Agree
4) Neutral/ Can't Tell
5) Somewhat Disagree
6) Disagree
7) Strongly Disagree

8. Is your company using professional business/ legal etc advisors?

1) Strongly Agree
2) Agree
3) Somewhat Agree
4) Neutral/ Can't Tell
5) Somewhat Disagree
6) Disagree
7) Strongly Disagree

9. Is your company started by people with tertiary education?

1) Strongly Agree
2) Agree
3) Somewhat Agree
4) Neutral/ Can't Tell
5) Somewhat Disagree
6) Disagree
7) Strongly Disagree

10. Is your company able to retain and attract good quality staff?

1) Strongly Agree
2) Agree
3) Somewhat Agree
4) Neutral/ Can't Tell
5) Somewhat Disagree
6) Disagree
7) Strongly Disagree

11. Is your company's products/ services very new or very old (have been in the market for a very long time)?

1) Strongly Agree
2) Agree
3) Somewhat Agree
4) Neutral/ Can't Tell
5) Somewhat Disagree
6) Disagree
7) Strongly Disagree

12. Was your company started during a period of economic boom/ uphill?

1) Strongly Agree
2) Agree
3) Somewhat Agree
4) Neutral/ Can't Tell
5) Somewhat Disagree
6) Disagree
7) Strongly Disagree

13. What was the age of the company founder when the company started?

1) Less than 20 years old
2) 21-40 years old
3) 41-60 years old
4) More than 60 years old

14. How many people/ partners started your company?

1) 1
2) 2
3) 3
4) More than 3

15. Are the parents of the company's owner(s) also business owners/entrepreneurs?

1) Strongly Agree
2) Agree
3) Somewhat Agree
4) Neutral/ Can't Tell
5) Somewhat Disagree
6) Disagree
7) Strongly Disagree

16. Is/ are the business owners of your company people with marketing skills?

1) Strongly Agree
2) Agree
3) Somewhat Agree
4) Neutral/ Can't Tell
5) Somewhat Disagree
6) Disagree
7) Strongly Disagree

17. Is your company owned by an ethnic minority?

1) Strongly Agree
2) Agree
3) Somewhat Agree
4) Neutral/ Can't Tell
5) Somewhat Disagree
6) Disagree
7) Strongly Disagree

18. Does your company enjoy good customer relationships?

1) Strongly Agree
2) Agree
3) Somewhat Agree
4) Neutral/ Can't Tell
5) Somewhat Disagree
6) Disagree
7) Strongly Disagree

19. Does your company have a niches market?

1) Strongly Agree
2) Agree
3) Somewhat Agree
4) Neutral/ Can't Tell
5) Somewhat Disagree
6) Disagree
7) Strongly Disagree

20. Does your company have a high business operating costs?

1) Strongly Agree
2) Agree
3) Somewhat Agree
4) Neutral/ Can't Tell
5) Somewhat Disagree
6) Disagree
7) Strongly Disagree

21. Does your company have the ability to develop & sustain technological edge(s)?

1) Strongly Agree
2) Agree
3) Somewhat Agree
4) Neutral/ Can't Tell
5) Somewhat Disagree
6) Disagree
7) Strongly Disagree

22. Does your company faces strong competition from rivals?

1) Strongly Agree
2) Agree
3) Somewhat Agree
4) Neutral/ Can't Tell
5) Somewhat Disagree
6) Disagree
7) Strongly Disagree

23. Does your company have strong top leadership?

1) Strongly Agree
2) Agree
3) Somewhat Agree
4) Neutral/ Can't Tell
5) Somewhat Disagree
6) Disagree
7) Strongly Disagree

24. Does your company have significant people bonding?

1) Strongly Agree
2) Agree
3) Somewhat Agree
4) Neutral/ Can't Tell
5) Somewhat Disagree
6) Disagree
7) Strongly Disagree

25. Does your company have strong organizational capability?

1) Strongly Agree
2) Agree
3) Somewhat Agree
4) Neutral/ Can't Tell
5) Somewhat Disagree
6) Disagree
7) Strongly Disagree

26. Does your company have access to broad support & resources?

1) Strongly Agree
2) Agree
3) Somewhat Agree
4) Neutral/ Can't Tell
5) Somewhat Disagree
6) Disagree
7) Strongly Disagree

27. Does your company have good local (Singaporean) market knowledge?

1) Strongly Agree
2) Agree
3) Somewhat Agree
4) Neutral/ Can't Tell
5) Somewhat Disagree
6) Disagree
7) Strongly Disagree

28. Do you think good government policy exist & benefited your company?

1) Strongly Agree
2) Agree
3) Somewhat Agree
4) Neutral/ Can't Tell
5) Somewhat Disagree
6) Disagree
7) Strongly Disagree

29. Which industry is your company in?

1)Manufacturing
2)Services
3)Agriculture

30. What products/ services does your company engage in?

1) Fast Moving Consumer Goods/products (FMCG)
2) Consumer Services
3) Industrial Goods
4) Industrial Services
5) Others

31. How many years has your company been in operation?

1) 1-3 years
2) 4-6 years
3) 7-9 years
4) 10-15 years
5) More than 15 years

32. How many employees do your company has?

1) 1-10 people
2) 11-50 people
3) 51-100 people
4) 101-200 people
5) More than 200 people

33. What are the average total assets of your company?

1) Less than S$1 million
2) Between S$1-5 million
3) Between S$5-10 million
4) Between S$10-15 million
5) More than S$ 15 million

34. How much is the average annual sales of your company?

1) Less than S$1 million
2) Between S$1-3 million
3) Between S$3-5 million
4) Between S$5-10 million
5) More than S$10 million

35. What is the percentage of your company's sale meant for exports?

1) Less than 5 percent
2) Between 5-10 percent
3) Between 10-30 percent
4) Between 30-50 percent
5) More than 50 percent

REFERENCES

Acs, Z., Morck,. R., Shaver, J., Yeung, B. (1997). "The Internationalization of Small and Medium-Sized Enterprises: A Policy Perspective." Small Business Economics 9: 7-20.

ADB (2003). "Catch-Up Competitiveness: Some Lessons." Asian Development Outlook 2003: III. Competitiveness in Developing Asia. Retrieved 9 Feb, 2009, from www.adb.org/Documents/Books/ADO/2003/part3_3-7.asp.

Anthony, R. N., Dearden, J., Vancil, R.F. (1972). Key Economic Variables, Irwin, Homewood, Illinois.

Antony, J., Dasai, D.A. (2009). "Assessing the status of six sigma implementation in the Indian industry." Management Research News 32(5): 413-423.

Anwar, S., Catley, B., Zheng, M. (2004). "Government Policies and the Growth of the Manufacturing Sector in Singapore." Journal of Business and Management 9(4): 373-388.

Anwar, S., Zheng, M. (2004). "Government spending on research and development and industrial production in Singapore " International Journal of Asian Management 3: 53-65.

Anwar, S. (2006). "Manufacturing Sector Growth: A Case Study of Singapore " Global Economic Review 35(4): 381-396.

Ashton, D. S., J. (1997). Education, skill formation and economic development: the Singaporean approach, in: Education: culture, economy and society. New York, Oxford University Press.

Asiaone News, Singapore. (2009). Singapore is 2nd Freest Economy. http://news.asiaone.com/print/News/Asiaone%2BNews/Singapore/Story/A12009011... (Accessed: 13 Jan 2009)

Aston, D., Green, F., Sung, J., James, D. (2002). "The Evolution of Education and Training Strategies in Singapore, Taiwan and S. Korea: a development model of skill formation." Journal of Education and Work 15(1): 5-30.

Atkinson, R. D., Andes,S.M. (2009). The Atlantic Century: Benchmarking EU & US Innovation and Competitiveness. A Information Technology & Innovation Foundation publication: Washington D.C.

Baker, E. W., Sinkula, J.M. (2009). "The Complementary Effects of Market Orientation and Entrepreneurial Orientation on Profitability in

Small Businesses." Journal of Small Business Management 47(4): 443-464.

Bamberger, I. (1989). "Developing Competitive Advantage in Small and Medium-size Firms." Long Range Planning 22(5): 80-88.

Bank, W. (2000). Improving Taxpayer Service and Facilitating Compliance in Singapore, World Bank.

Beaver, G., Price, C. (2004). "Management, Strategy and Policy in the UK Small Business Sector: A Critical Review." Journal of Small Business and Enterprise Development 11(1): 34-49.

Bender, R., Benner, A. (2000). "Calculating Ordinal Regression Models in SAS and S-Plus." Biometrical Journal 42(6): 677-699.

Benzing, C., Chu, H. M., Szabo, B. (2005). "Hungarian and Romanian Entrepreneurs in Romania: Motivation, Problems, and Differences." Journal of Global Business 16: 77-87.

Benzing, C., Chu, H. M., Bove, R. (2005). "The Motivation, Problems, and Perceived Success of Entrepreneurs in Romania." Journal of the Academy of Business Administration 10(1&2, Spring & Fall): 73–88.

Benzing, C., Chu, M.H., Callanan, G. (2005). "Regional Comparison of the Motivation and Problems of Vietnamese Entrepreneurs." Journal of Developmental Entrepreneurship 10: 3-27.

Benzing, C., Chu, H.M., Kara, O. (2009). "Entrepreneurs in Turkey: A Factor Analysis of Motivations, Success Factors, and Problems." Journal of Small Business Management 47(1): 58-91.

Bernroider, E. (2002). "Factors in SWOT Analysis Applied to Micro, Small-to-Medium, and Large Software Enterprises: An Austrian Study." European Management Journal 20(5): 562-573.

Berranger, P., Tucker, D., Jones, L. (2001). "Internet Diffusion in Creative Micro-Businesses: Identifying Change Agent Characteristics As Critical Success Factors." Journal of Organizational Computing and Electronic Commerce 11(3): 197-214.

Bianchi, C., Bivona, E. (Fall 2002). "Opportunities and Pitfalls Related to E-commerce Strategies in Small and Medium Firms: A System Dynamics Approach." System Dynamics Review 18(3): 403-429.

Bliss, R. T., Garratt, N.L. (2001). "Supporting Women Entrepreneurs in Transitioning Economies." Journal of Small Business Management 39(4): 336-344.

Blumentritt, T., Danis, W.M. (2006). "Business Strategy Types and Innovation Practices." Journal of Managerial Issues 18(2): 274-291.

Buckley, P. (1989). "Foreign Direct Investment by Small and Medium Sized Enterprises: The Theoretical Background." Small Business Economics 1: 89-100.

Burns, P., Harrison, J. (1996). Growth, Macmillan Press Ltd.

Busch, E. T. (1989). "Small Business Hurdles in Ecuador." Journal of Small Business Management 27(1): 70-73. Business Environment Risk Intelligence (BERI) http://beri.com/ (Accessed: 5 July 2010)

Butler, T., Fitzgerald, B. (1999). "Unpacking the Systems Development Process: An Empirical Application of the CSF Concept in a Research Context." Journal of Strategic Information System 8(4): 351-371.

Cagliano, R., Blackmon, K., Voss, C. (2001). "Small Firms under MICROSCOPE: International Differences in Production/ Operations Management Practices and Performance." Integrated Manufacturing Systems 12(7): 469-482.

Camillo, A., Connolly, D., Kim, W. G. (2008). "Success and failure in Northern California: critical success factors for independent restaurants." Cornell Hospitality Quarterly 49(4): 364-380.

Campos, J. E., Gonzalez III, J.L. (1999). "Deliberation Councils, Government -Business-Citizen Partnerships, and Public Policy-Making: Cases from Singapore, Malaysia and Canada." Asia Pacific Journal of Management 16: 429-447.

Carlberg, J., Ward, C., Holcomb, R. (2004) Success Factors for New Generation Cooperatives. Oklahoma Cooperative Extension Service AGEC-596, 1-7

Carlsson, B., Mudambi, R. (2003). "Globalization, Entrepreneurship, and Public Policy: A Systems View." Industry and Innovation 10(1): 103-116.

Cavana, R., Delahaye, B. & Sekaran, U. (2001). Applied Business Research: Qualitative and Quantitative Research. Sydney, John Wiley & Sons Australia.

Channel News Asia, Singapore. (2008). Managerial Talent in SMEs. http://www.channelnewsasia.com/advertorial/businessleaders/ (Accessed: 17 Nov 2008)

Channel News Asia, Singapore. (2008). 21 November 2008. Singapore Government to Provide Extra S$2.3 billion in Loan Support to Businesses. http://www.channelnewsasia.com/stories/singaporelocalnews/view/391267/1/.html (Accessed: 21 Nov 2008)

Channel News Asia, Singapore (2009). 9 February 2009. Trade Minister says Singapore Poised to Weather Downturn. http://www.channelnewsasia.com/stories/singaporelocalnews/print/407777/1/.html (Accessed: 10 Feb 2009)

Channel News Asia, Singapore. (2008). 21 November 2008. Singapore Government Allocates S$600 million for Skills Upgrading. http://

www.channelnewsasia.com/singaporelocalnews/view/391279/1/.html (Accessed: 21 Nov 2008)

Channel News Asia, Singapore. (2009). Singapore Taps Reserves for S$20.5 b Economic Stimulus Plan. Available from http://www.sg.news.yahoo.com/cna/20090122/tap-182-singapore-govt-introduce-s-20-5b-23165 (Accessed: 23 Jan 2009)

Channel News Asia, Singapore. 3 May 2009. SPUR-JOBS to provide up to S$400k in co-funding recruitment, training. http: www.channelnewsasia.com/stories/singaporelocalnews/print/426652/1/.html (Accessed: 4 May 2009)

Chen, C. K., Hughes, J. Jr (2004). "Using Ordinal Regression Model to Analyse Student Satisfaction Questionnaires." IR Applications Using Advance Tools, Techniques & Methodologies 1.

Cheng, H. L., Lin, C.Y.Y. (2009). "Do as the Large Enterprises do? Expatriate Selection and Overseas Performance in Emerging Markets: The Case of Taiwan SMEs." International Business Review 18: 60-75.

Chu, H. M., Benzing, C., McGee, C. (2007). "Ghanaian and Kenyan Entrepreneurs: A Comparative Analysis of Their Motivations, Success Characteristics, and Problems." Journal of Developmental Entrepreneurship 12(3): 295–322.

Commission, E. "Definition of SME." Available from http://ec.europa.eu/enterprise/enterprise_policy/sme_definition/index_en.htm. (Accessed: 21 May 2008)

Conant, J. S., Mokwa M.P., Varadarajan, P.R. (1990). "Strategic Types, Distinctive Marketing Competencies and Organizational Performance: A Multiple Measures-Based Study." Strategic Management Journal 11: 365-383.

Covin, J. G., Slevin, D. P. (1989). "Strategic Management of Small Firms in Hostile and Benign Environments." Strategic Management Journal 10: 75-87.

Covin, J. G., Covin, T. J. (1990). "Competitive Aggressiveness, Environmental Context and Small Firm Performance." EntrepreneurshipTheory and Practice: 35-50.

Coy, S. P., Shipley, M. F., Omer, K. Rao, N. A. (2007). "Factors Contributory to Success: A Study of Pakistan's Small Business Owners." Journal of Developmental Entrepreneurship 12(2): 189-198.

Cunningham, J. B. (1995). "Success in Corporate and Entrepreneurial Organizations in Singapore." Journal of Small Business Management October: 80-86.

Daniel, D. R. (1961). "Management Information Crisis." Harvard Business Review (Sep-Oct): 110-119.

Danis, W. M., Chiaburu, D. S., Lyles, M. A. (2010). "The Impact of Managerial Networking Intensity and Market-based Strategies on Firm Growth during Institutional Upheaval: A Study of small and medium-sized Enterprises in a Transition Economy." Journal of International Business Studies 41: 287-307.

DeHayes, D. W. a. H., W.L. (1990). University Alumni Small Business Research Program: A Study of Emerging Businesses. Centre for Entrepreneurship and Innovation, Indiana University.

Demirbag, M., Tatoglu, E., Glaister, K.W. (2007). "Factors Influencing Perceptions of Performance: The Case of Western FDI in an Emerging Market." International Business Review 16: 310-336.

Dess, G. G., Lumpkin, G. T., Covin, J. G. (1997). "Entrepreneurial Strategy Making and Firm Performance: Tests of Contingency and Configuration Models." Strategic Management Journal 18(9): 677–695.

Dillman, D. A. (1978). Mail and telephone surveys: the total design method New York: Wiley

—. (2000). Mail and internet surveys: the tailored design method New York, New York: J. Wiley.

Dutta, S., Evrard, P. (1999). "Information Technology and Organisation within European Small Enterprises." European Management Journal 17(3): 239-251.

Edwards, T., Delbridge, R., Munday, M. (2005). "Understanding Innovation in Small and Medium-sized Enterprises: A Process Manifest." Technovation 25: 1119-1127.

Economic Development Board Singapore. (2009). Singapore is the World's Easiest Place to do business. http://www.sedb.com./edb/sg/en_uk/index/why_singapore/Singapore_rankings.html (Accessed: 30 Jun 2009)

Economic Development Board Singapore. (2010). http://www.edb.gov.sg (Accessed: 8 Oct 2010)

Enriquez, M. 6 April 2010. A Grant to help businesses become more family-friendly. Today (Singapore Newspaper). Singapore Press Holdings.

European Network for SME Research (ENSR) (1995). The European Observatory for SMEs (3rd Annual Report). Zoetermeer, the Netherlands: ENSR.

Feindt, S., Jeffcoate, J., Chappell, C. (2002). "Identifying Success Factors for Rapid Growth in SME E-commerce." Journal of Small Business Economics 19: 51-62.

Filatotchev, I., Liu, X.H., Buck, T., Wright, M. (2009). "The Export Orientation and Export Performance of High-Technology SMEs in

Emerging Markets: The Effects of Knowledge Transfer by Returnee Entrepreneurs." Journal of International Business Studies 40: 1005-1021.

Fischer, E., Reuber, A.R. (2002). "Support for Rapid Growth Firms: A Comparison of the Views of Founders, Government Policy Makers and Private Sector Resource Providers." Journal of Small Business Management.

Francis, J., Mukherji, A., Mukherji, J. (2009). "Examining Relational and Resource Influences on the Performance of Border Region SMEs." International Business Review 18: 331-343.

Frese, M., A. Brantjes., R. Hoorn (2002). "Psychological Success Factors of Small Scale Businesses in Namibia: The Roles of Strategy Process, Entrepreneurial Orientation and the Environment,"." Journal of Developmental Entrepreneurship 7(3): 259-282.

Frost, F. A. (2003). "The Use of Strategic Tools by small and medium-sized enterprises: An Australasian Study." Strategic Change 12(Jan-Feb): 49-62.

Friel, C.M. (2009). "Notes on Factor Analysis." Criminal Justice Center, Sam Houston State University. www.shsu.edu/~icc_cmf/cj_742/stats9.doc (Accessed: 17 Aug 2010)

Gadenne, D. (1998). "Critical Success Factors for Small Business: An Inter-industry Comparison." International Small Business Journal 17(1): 36-56.

Garson, G. D. (2009). "Logistic Regression: Statnotes from North Carolina State University". http://faculty.chass.ncsu.edu/garson/PA765/logistic.htm. (Accessed: 10 Nov 2009)

Garson, G. D. (2009). "Ordinal Regression: Statnotes from North Carolina State University." http://faculty.chass.ncsu.edu/garson/PA765/ordinalreg.htm. (Accessed: 10 Nov 2009)

Gengatharen, D. E., Standing, C. (2005). "A Framework to Assess the Factors Affecting Success or Failure of the Implementation of Government-supported Regional E-marketplaces for SMEs." European Journal of Information Systems 14: 417-433.

Ghesquiere, H. (2006). Singapore's Success: Engineering Economic Growth, Thomson Learning.

Ghosh, B. C., Kwan, W. (1996). An Analysis of Key Success Factors of SMEs: A Cross National Study of Singapore/Malaysia and Australia/New Zealand, ICSB, Sweden.

Ghosh, B. C., Tan, W.L., Tan, T.M., Chan, B. (2001). "The Key Success Factors, Distinctive Capabilities and Strategic Thrusts of Top SMEs in Singapore." Journal of Business Research 51: 209-221.

Gill, J. (2000). Generalized Linear Model: A Unified Approach. California: Sage Publication, Thousand Oaks.

Gilmore, A., Carson, D., Rocks, S. (2006). "Networking in SMEs: Evaluating its Contribution to Marketing Activity." International Business Review 15: 278-293.

Goh, E. G., F. (1997). "Trade unions as agents for skill formation: the case of Singapore." International Journal of Training and Development 1(4): 230–241.

Gosh, B. C., T. S. Kim., L. A. Meng (1993). "Factors Contributing to the Success of Local SMEs: An Insight from Singapore." Journal of Small Business and Entrepreneurship 10(3): 33-45.

Graham, P. G. (1999). "Small Business Participation in the Global Economy." European Journal of Marketing 33(1/2): 88-102.

Greenlan, S. (1994). "Alternative Models for Ordinal Logistic Regression." Statistics in Medicine 13: 1665-1677.

Group, D. I. (2009). Singapore 1000. D. I. Group. Singapore: 286.

—. (2009). Singapore SME 500. D. I. Griup: 150.

Gujarati, D. (2006). Essentials of Econometrics. New York, McGraw-Hill/ Irwin.

Gumede, V., Rasmussen, K. (2002). "Small Manufacturing Enterprises and Exporting in South Africa: A Preliminary Assessment of Key Export Success Factors." Journal of Small Business and Enterprise Development 9(2): 162-171.

Etemad, H. R. W., Ed. (2001). Globalization and Entrepreneurship, McGill.

Hadjimanolis, A. (1999). "Barriers to Innovation for SMEs in a small less Developed Country." Technovation(19): 561-570.

Harding, R. (2000). "Venture Capital and Regional Development: Towards a Venture Capital 'System'." Venture Capital 2(4): 287-311.

Headd, B., Kirchhoff, B. (2009). "The Growth, Decline and Survival of Small Businesses: An Exploratory Study of Life Cycles." Journal of Small Business Management 47(4): 531-550.

Henderson, R., Robertson, M (2000). "Who Wants to be an Entrepreneur? Young Adult Attitudes to Entrepreneurship as a Career." Career Development International 5/6: 279-287.

Hew, D., Loi, W. N. Ed. (2004). Entrepreneurship and SMEs in Southeast Asia Institute of Southeast Asian Studies.

Hewitt, S. (1997). "Business Excellence: Does it Work for Small Companies." The TQM Magazine 9(1): 76-82.
Hill, H. (2001). "Small and Medium Enterprises in Indonesia." Asian Survey 41(2): 248-270.
Hodgkinson, G. P. (2001). "The Psychology of Strategic Management: Diversity and Cognition Revisited." International Review of Industrial and Organizational Psychology 16: 65-119.
Hofer, C. W., Schendel, D.E. (1978). Strategy Formulation: Analytical Concepts. St. Paul, Minn., West Publications Inc.
Hoffmann, W. H., Schlosser, R. (2001). "Success Factors of Strategic Alliances in Small and Medium-sized Enterprises: An Empirical Survey." Long Range Planning 34: 357-381.
Hogg, S., Medway, D., Warnaby, G. (2003). "Business Improvement Districts: An Opportunity for SME Retailing." International Journal of Retail & Distribution Management 31(9): 466-469.
Hopkins, M. (1997). Help Wanted. Inc. Boston, MA. 19.
Hosmer, D.W., Lemeshow, S. (1989). Applied Logistic Regression. New York: John Wiley & Sons
Huck, J. F., McEwen, T. (1991). "Competencies needed for small business success: Perceptions of Jamaican Entrepreneurs." Journal of Small Business Management 29(4): 90-93.
Huff, W. G. (1995). "The developmental state, government, and Singapore's economic development since 1960." World Development 23(8): 1421–1438.
Ibrahim, A. B., Goodwin, J. R. (1986). "Perceived Causes of Success in Small Business." American Journal of Small Business Fall (41-50).
IMD World Competitiveness Yearbook 2010 http://www.imd.ch/research/publications/wcy/upload/scoreboard.pdf (Accessed: 5 July 2010)
International Enterprise Singapore. (2010). http: www.iesingapore.gov.sg (Accessed: 8 Oct 2010)
—. (2010). IE Singapore Work Plan Seminar Report 2010 on 'Summary of Small & Mighty Enterprises'. Singapore, IE Singapore.
International Enterprise Singapore, S. S., Singapore Workforce Development Agency (2010). Key Government Assistance Programmes for SMEs. Singapore, Spring Singapore.
IRAS (2010). Inland Revenue Authority of Singapore. Available from http: www.iras.gov.sg (Accessed: 23 Nov 2010).
Jeffcoate, J., Chappell, C., Feindt, S. (2000). "Attitude Towards Process Improvement among SMEs Involved in E-commerce." Knowledge and Process Management 7(3): 187-195.

Jennex, M. E., Amoroso, D. (2004). "E-Commerce Infrastructure Success Factors for Small Companies in Developing Economies." Electronic Commerce Research 4: 263-286.

Jenster, P. V. (1987). "Using Critical Success Factors in Planning." Long Range Planning 20(4): 102-109.

Jeon, B. N., Han, K.S., Lee, M.J. (2006). "Determining Factors for the Adoption of E-business: the Case of SMEs in Korea." Applied Economics 38: 1905-1916.

Kamal, M. M. (2006). "IT Innovation Adoption in the Government Sector: Identifying the Critical Success Factors." Journal of Enterprise Information Management 19(2): 192-222.

Kim, J., Lau, L. (1994). "The Sources of Economic Growth in the Newly Industrialised Countries." The Journal of the Japanese and International Economies 8: 235-271.

Kim, Y., Lee, K. (2003). "Technological Collaboration in the Korean Electronic Parts Industry: Patterns and Key Success Factors." R & D Management 33(1): 59-77.

Koop, S., T. De Reu, M. Frese (2000). Socio-Demographic Factors, Entrepreneurial Orientation, Personal Initiative and Environmental Problems in Uganda. Westport, CT, Quorum.

Kozan, M. K., Oksoy, D.,Ozsoy, O. (2006). "Growth Plans of Small Business in Turkey: Individual and Environmental Influences." Journal of Small Business Management 4(11): 114–129.

Krause, L. (1987). The Singapore Economy Reconsidered. Singapore, Institute of Southeast Asian Studies.

Kumar, M. (2007). "Explaining Entrepreneurial Success: A Conceptual Model." Academy of Entrepreneurship Journal 13(1): 57-77.

Lau, G. T., Lim, J.W.B (1996). "An Exploratory Study of Factors Affecting the Failure of Local Small and Medium Enterprises." Asia Pacific Journal of Management 13(2): 47-61.

Lawton, T. C. (2002). "Missing the target: Assessing the Role of Government in bridging the European Equity Gap and Enhancing Economic Growth." Venture Capital 4(1): 7-23.

Leaptrott, J., McDonald, J.M. (2008). "Looking Before Leaping: The Effect of Owner Decisiveness on Small Business Performance." Academy of Entrepreneurship Journal 14(1): 1-12.

Lee, K. Y. (1999). The Singapore Story: Memoirs of Lee Kuan Yew, Prentice Hall.

—. (2000). From Third World to First: The Singapore Story: 1965-2000, Harper Collins.

Lee, S. S., Stearns, T.M., Osteryoung, J.S., Stephenson, H.B. (2009). "A comparison of the critical success factors in women-owned business between the United States and Korea." International Entrepreneurship and Management Journal.

Leidecker, J. K., Bruno, A.V. (1984). "Identifying and Using Critical Success Factors." Long Range Planning 17(Feb): 23-32.

Lerner, M., Haber, S. (2000). "Performance Factors of Small Tourism Ventures: The Interface of Tourism, Entrepreneurship and the Environment." Journal of Business Venturing 16: 77-100.

Levy, M., Powell, P. (2003). "Exploring SME Internet Adoption: Towards a Contingent Model." Electronic Markets 13(2): 173-181.

Lin, C. Y. Y. (1998). "Success Factors of Small and Medium-sized Enterprises in Taiwan: An Analysis of Cases." Journal of Small Business Management 36(4): 43-57.

Lofsten, H., Lindelof, P. (2002). "Science Parks and the Growth of New Technology-based Firms - Academic-Industry links, Innovation and Markets." Research Policy 31: 859-876.

Lowe, P., Talbot, H. (2000). "Policy for Small Business Support in Rural Areas: A Critical Assessment of the Proposal for the Small Business Service " Regional Studies 34(5): 479-499.

Lussier, R. N. (1995). "A Non-Financial Business Success Versus Failure Prediction Model for Young Firms." Journal of Small Business Management 33(1): 8-20.

Lussier, R. N., Pfeifer, S. (2000). "A Comparison of Business Success versus Failure Variables between U.S. and Central Eastern Europe Croatian Entrepreneurs." Entrepreneurship Theory and Practice 24(4): 59-67.

Lussier, R. N., Pfeifer, S. (2001). "A Crossnational Prediction Model for Business Success." Journal of Small Business Management 39(3): 228-239.

Lussier, R. N. (2005). "A Success Versus Failure Prediction Model for the Real Estate Industry." Mid-American Journal of Business 20(1): 47-53.

Lussier, R. N., Sonfield, M.C. (2007). "A Comparison of Family-Member & Non-Family-Member Managers in American Family Business." Academy of Entrepreneurship Journal 13(2): 31-46.

Man, T. W. Y., Lau, T., Chan, K.F. (2002). "The Competitiveness of Small and Medium Enterprises: A Conceptualization with Focus on Entrepreneurial Competencies." Journal of Business Venturing 17: 123-142.

Maxwell, J.A. (2005). Qualitative Research Design: An Interactive Approach (2nd Ed). Thousand Oaks: Sage Publication.

Maysami, R. C., Goby, V.P. (1999). "Female business owners in Singapore and elsewhere: a review of studies." Journal of Small Business Management 37(2): 96-105.

McAdam, R., Kelly, M. (2002). "A Business Excellence Approach to Generic Benchmarking in SMEs." Benchmarking: An International Journal 9(1): 7-27.

McCullagh, P., Nelder, J.A. (1989). Generalized Linear Models. New York: Chapman and Hall.

Ministry of Finance, S. (2009). Beyond Stewardship: 50 Years of the MOF 1959-2009. Ministry of Finance, Singapore.

—. (2009). "Singapore Government Allocates S$600 million for Skills Upgrading." www.channelnewsasia.com/stories/singaporelocalnews/print/391279/1/.html (Accessed: 21 Nov 2008).

—. (2009). "Singapore Taps Reserves for S$20.5 b Economic Stimulus Plan." www.channelnewsasis.com. (Accessed: 23 Jan 2009).

Ministry of Manpower, S. (2008). Singapore Manpower Report 2008. Singapore, Singapore Ministry of Manpower: 1-68.

Ministry of Trade & Industry, S. (2009). "Trade Minister says Singapore Poised to Weather Downturn." www.channelnewsasia.com/stories/singaporelocalnews/print/407777/1/.html (Accessed: 20 Feb 2009).

Mole, K. (2000). "Gambling for Growth or Settling for Survival: The Dilemma of the Small Business Adviser." Journal of Small Business and Enterprise Development 7(4): 305-314.

Monetary Authority of Singapore (MAS). 2010. *Singapore International Financial Center: Gateway to Opportunities in Asia and Beyond* www.mas.gov.sg (Accessed: 2 Oct 2010).

Montes, F. M., Giap, T. K., Ed. (1999). Developing the financial services industry in Singapore. East Asia's Financial Systems: Evolution and Crisis. Singapore, NRI/ISEAS.

Neo, B. S., Chen, G. (2007). Dynamic Governance: Embedding Culture, Capabilities and Change in Singapore. Singapore, World Scientific.

Neshamba, F. (2000). Growth and Transformation Among Small Business in Kenya. Nottingham, UK, The Nottingham Trent University.

Ngiam, T. D. (2006). A Mandarin and the Making of Public Policy: Reflections by Ngiam Tong Dow. Singapore, NUS Press.

—. (2011). Dynamics of the Singapore Success Story: Insights by Ngiam Tong Dow. Singapore, Cengage Learning Asia.

Nijkamp, P. (2003). "Entrepreneurship in a Modern Network Economy." Regional Studies 37(4): 395-405.

Ojala, A. (2009). "Internationalization of Knowledge-Intensive SMEs: The Role of Network Relationships in the Entry to a Psychically Distant Market." International Business Review 18: 50-59.

Olson, P. D., Bokor, D. W. (1995). "Strategy Process-Content Interaction: Effects on Growth Performance in Small, Start Up Firms." Journal of Small Business Management 33(1): 34-44.

Parayil, G. (2005). "From “Silicon Island” to “Biopolis of Asia”: Innovation Policy and Shifting Competitive Strategy in Singapore." California Management Review 47(2): 50-73.

Parker, R. (2000). "Small is not Necessarily Beautiful: An Evaluation of Policy Support for Small and Medium-sized Enterprises in Australia." Australian Journal of Political Science 35(2): 239-253.

Perry, C. (1998). "A Structured approach to presenting theses." 2009, from www.scu.edu.au/schools/gcm/ar/art/cperry.html.

Petroni, A. (2002). "Critical Factors of MRP Implementation in Small and Medium-sized Firms." International Journal of Operations & Production Management 22(3): 329-348.

Plank, S.B., Jordan, W.J. (1997). Reducing Talent Loss. The Impact of Information, Guidance, and Actions on Postsecondary Enrollment. Eric No: ED405429.

Portal, E. (2009). "SME Infocomm Resources Centre@ Singapore Polytechnic (SIRC@SP)." www.business.gov.sg. (Accessed: 23 July 2009).

Portal, S. S. (2008). "SME Definition." from http://www.singapore-sme.com/aboutus.asp.

Powell, P., Levy, M. (2000). "Information Systems Strategy for Small and Medium-sized Enterprises: An Organizational Perspective." Journal of Strategic Information System 9: 63-84.

Pratt, V. (2001). "Sharing Business Skills in Kenya." from http://www.cipe.org. (Accessed: 26 December 2009).

Press, A.-F. (2009). Singapore is 2nd Freest Economy Agence-France Press 13 Jan 2009.

Pun, K. F., Chin, K.S., White, A.S., Gill, R. (2004). "Determinants of Manufacturing Strategy Formulation: A longitudinal Study in Hong Kong." Technovation 24: 121-137.

Rajan, R. S., Ed. (2003). Sustaining Competitiveness in the New Global Economy : The Experience of Singapore Institute of Policy Studies, Singapore, Cheltenham, UK ; Northampton, MA : Edward Elgar Pub.

Rauch, A., Frese, M., Ed. (1998). A Contingency Approach to Small Scale Business Success: A Longitudinal Study on the Effects of Environmental Hostility and Uncertainty on the Relationship between

Planning and Success. Frontiers of Entrepreneurship Research. Babson Park, MA, Babson College Press.

Reid, R., Morrow, T., Kelly, B., McCartan, P. (2002). "People Management in SMEs: An Analysis of Human Resource Strategies in Family and Non-family Businesses." Journal of Small Business and Enterprise Development 9(3): 245-259.

Rockart, J. F. (1979). "Chief Executives define their own Data Needs." Harvard Business Review (Mar-Apr): 81-92.

Rodan, G. (2001). Singapore: Globalisation and the politics of economic restructuring. Oxford, Oxford University Press.

Rungasamy, S., Antony, F., Ghosh, S. (2002). "Critical Success Factors for SPC implementation in UK small and medium enterprises: some key findings from a survey." The TQM Magazine 14(4): 217-224.

Sadler-Smith, E., Hampson, Y., Chaston, I., Badger, B. (2003). "Managerial Behaviour, Entrepreneurial Style and Small Firm Performance." Journal of Small Business Management 41(1): 47-67.

Schein, E. H. (1996). Strategic Pragmatism: The Culture of Singapore's Economics Development Board. Singapore, Toppan Company Singapore Private Limited.

Scherr, F.C. (1989). "Causality, Regression, Discriminant Analysis and Research on Failure." Akron Business and Economic Review (Spring), 8-20.

Scott, S. C., Goldberg, Mark S., and Mayo, Nancy E. (1997). "Statistical Assessment of Ordinal Outcomes in Comparative Studies." Clinical Epidemiology 50(1): 45-55.

Sebora, T. C., Lee, S.M., Sukasame, N. (2009). "Critical success factors for e-commerce entrepreneurship: an empirical study of Thailand." Small Business Economics 32(3): 303-316.

Shapiro, H. (2007). Industrial Policy and Growth. UN DESA Working Paper No. 63, United Nations: 1-15.

Sherer, S. A. (2003). "Critical Success Factors for Manufacturing Networks as Perceived by Network Coordinators." Journal of Small Business Management 41(4): 325-345.

Sila I., E., M. (2003). "Examination and Comparison of the Critical Factors of Total Quality Management (TQM) Across Countries." International Journal of Production Research 41(2): 235-268.

Simpson, M., Tuck, M., Bellamy, S. (2004). "Small business success factors: the role of education and training." Education & Training 46(8/9): 481-491.

Singapore SME Portal. (2010). Definition of an SME in Singapore. Available from http://www.singapore-sme.com/aboutus.htm (Accessed: 13 Oct 2010)

Singapore, Y. P. (2008/2009). Yellow Pages Singapore Buying Guide. Y. P. Singapore. Singapore, Yellow Pages Singapore: 652.

Spring Singapore. (2010). http:www.spring.gov.sg (Accessed: 8 Oct 2010).

—. (2009). "Spring Singapore Launches $30 million Incubator Development Programme." http://www.spring.gov.sg/Content/PrintPage.aspx?group=nw&id=5518ff88-7d44-442. (Accessed: 24 Feb 2009).

—. (2009). Speech by Mr Lee Yi Shyan, Minister of State for Trade and Industry at the Spring SEEDS Conference in 2009. http://www.spring.gov.sg/Content/ModulePage.aspx?group=nw&id=4d746399-2d0d-4b9d-834c-bfc74a4a255b (Accessed: 24 Feb 2009).

—. (2009). Spring Builds Local Enterprises for the Future. http://www.spring.gov.sg/Content/ModulePage.aspx?group=nw&id=385b8db0-56dc-4e81-bf50-67c98ba4e9a8 (Accessed: 24 Feb 2009).

—. (2009). Spring Singapore Launches $30 million Incubator Development Programme. http:www.spring.gov.sg/Content/PrintPage.aspx?group=nw&id=5518ff88-7d44-442 (Accessed: 24 Feb 2009).

—. (2008). SME Development Report 2008. Available at http://www.spring.gov.sg/Content/WebPage.aspx?id=0e7aee48-13fc-4a68-91f7-14e053a68523 (Accessed: 15 Nov 2008).

SME Committee (1989). SME Master Plan: Report on Enterprise Development. Singapore: EDB, 1989.

SME 21 Committee (2000). SME 21: Positioning SMEs for the 21st Century. Singapore: PSB, 2000.

Sonfield, M., Lussier, R., Corman, J., McKinney, M. (2001). "Gender Comparisons in Strategic Decision-Making: An Empirical Analysis of the Entrepreneurial Strategy Matrix." Journal of Small Business Management 39(2): 165-173.

Sparkes, A., Thomas, B. (2001). "The use of the Internet as a critical success factor for the marketing of Welsh agri-food SMEs in the Twenty-first century." British Food Journal 103(5): 331-347.

SPSS (2008). Guide to SPSS 16.0. SPSS Corporation.

Statistics.com (2009). "Logistic Regression." (Accessed: 6 Nov 2009).

Statistics Singapore (2010). www.singstat.gov.sg (Accessed: 8 Sep 2010)

Storey, D. J. (1994). Understanding the Small Business Sector. London, Routledge.

Sum, C. C., Kow, L.S.J., Chen, C.S. (2004). "A Taxonomy of Operations Strategies of High Performing small and medium enterprises in Singapore." International Journal of Operations & Production Management 24(3): 321-345.

Sung, J. (2006). Explaining the Economic Success of Singapore: The Developmental Worker as the Missing Link. Surrey, Edward Elgar Publishing.

Survey, S. D. (2007). "Joint Statement by Spring Singapore, International Enterprise Singapore & Infocomm Development Authority of Singapore on the SME Development Survey 2007." http://www.dpgroup.com.sg/news/press/2007/doc/Joint%20Media%20Statement%20SME%20Devt%20Survey%202007%20-%2019Sep07.doc. (Accessed: 26 August 2008).

Tambunan, T. (2005). "Promoting Small and Medium Enterprises with a Clustering Approach: A Policy Experience from Indonesia." Journal of Small Business Management 43(2): 138-154.

Tan, K. C., Chakrabarty, A. (2009). "An exploratory qualitative and quantitative analysis of Six Sigma in service organizations in Singapore." Management Research News 32(7): 614-632.

Tang, Z., Kreiser, P.M., Marino, L., Weaver, K.M. (2010). "Exploring Proactiveness as a Moderator in the Process of Perceiving Industrial Munificence: A Field Study of SMEs in Four Countries." Journal of Small Business Management 48(2): 97-115.

Taylor, A. (2005). "An Operations Perspective on Strategic Alliance Success Factors: An Exploratory Study of Alliance Managers in the Software Industry." International Journal of Operations & Production Management 25(5): 469-490.

Taylor, M., Murphy, A. (2004). "SMEs and e-business." Journal of Small Business and Enterprise Development 11(3): 280-289.

Temtime, Z. T., Solomon, G.H. (2002). "Total Quality Management and the Planning Behaviour of SMEs in Developing Economies." TQM Magazine 14(3): 181-191.

Teng, S.S., Bhatia, G.S. & Anwar, S. (2011). "A Success versus Failure Prediction Model for Small Businesses in Singapore." American Journal of Business 26(1): 50-64.

Tetteh, E., Burn, J. (2001). "Global Strategies for SMe-business: Applying the SMALL Framework." Logistic Information Management 14(1/2): 171-180.

Tharenou, P., Donohue, R. & Cooper, B. (2007). "Management Research Methods." Melbourne: Cambridge University Press.

The Business Times Singapore. 24 July 2009. Help for SMEs to Tap Internet for Growth. Singapore Press Holdings.

The Straits Times. 2 May 2009. 54,000 firms get aid to expand globally. Singapore Press Holdings.

—. 3 July 2009. Rise of the New Entrepreneur. Singapore Press Holdings.

—. 29 July 2009. Bosses go back to school to learn biz management. Singapore Press Holdings.

—. 26 June 2009. Diverse line-up for growth ideas. Singapore Press Holdings.

—. 17 April 2009. Doing Business? Singapore is Fourth Best. Singapore Press Holdings.

—. 11 April 2009. Government Initiatives (SPUR & Jobs Credit Scheme).Singapore Press Holdings.

—. 16 April 2009. Government-backed Loans Double in a Month. Singapore Press Holdings.

—. 28 March 2009. Jobless? Be an SME Adviser. Singapore Press Holdings.

Thomas, R., Long, J. (2000). "Improving Competitiveness: Critical Success Factors for Tourism Development." Local Economy 14(4): 313-329.

Tsao, H. Y., Lin, K.H.C., Lin, C. (2004). "An Investigation of Critical Success Factors in the Adoption of B2BEC by Taiwanese Companies." The Journal of American Academy of Business, Cambridge(Sept): 198-202.

Tung, R. L., Aycan, Z. (2008). "Key Factors and Indigenous Management Practices in SMEs in Emerging Economies." Journal of World Business 43: 381-384.

United States Government Printing Office (1995). *The State of Small Business: A Report of the President*. Washington, DC: U.S. Government Printing Office.

Valsamakis, V. P., Sprague, L.G. (2001). "The Role of Customer Relationships in the Growth of small to medium-sized Manufacturers." International Journal of Operations & Production Management 24(1): 427-445.

Voudouris, I., Lioukas, S., Makridakis, S., Spanos, Y. (2000). "Greek Hidden Champions: Lessons from Small, Little-known Firms in Greece." European Management Journal 18(6): 663-674.

Wade, R. (1990). Governing the Market: Economic Theory & the Role of Government in East Asian Industrialization. New Jersey, Princeton University Press.

Wagner, B. A., Fillis, I., Johansson, U. (2003). "E-business and E -supply Strategy in Small and Medium-sized Businesses (SMEs)." Supply Chain Management 8(4): 343-354.

Walters, S.J., Campbell, M.J., Lall, R. (2001). “Design and Analysis of Trials with Quality of Life as an Outcome: A practical Guide.” Journal of Biopharmaceutical Statistics 11(3): 155-176.

Wilkinson, T., Brouthers, L. E. (2006). "Trade Promotion and SME Export Performance." International Business Review 15: 233-252.

Wooldridge, J. M. (2000). Introductory Econometrics. South-Western College Publishing.

World Bank. (2010). Economy Rankings. http: www.doingbusiness.org/Rankings (Accessed: 25 Oct 2010).

World Bank Database (2010) on Singapore’s Per Capita GDP available at www.worldbank.org (Accessed: 7 Sep 2010).

Yap, S., Lim, R., Leong, W.K., Ed. (2009). Men In White. Singapore, Marshall Cavendish.

Yearbook of Statistics Singapore 2010. Available from http://www.singstat.gov.sg/pubn/catalogue.html. (Accessed: 29 Sep 2010)

Yeung, H. W.-C., Chew, Y.T. (2001). "The SME Advantage: Adding Local Touch to Foreign Transnational Corporations in Singapore." Regional Studies 35(5): 431-448.

Yoshi, T., Nham, P.T. (2009). "Factors Contributing to the Growth of Small and Medium Enterprises: An Empirical Analysis of Vietnam’s Manufacturing Firms." Singapore Management Review 31(2): 35-51.

Yusuf, A. (1995). "Critical Success Factors for Small Business: Perceptions of South Pacific Entrepreneurs." Journal of Small Business Management 33(2): 68-73.

Zapalska, A. (1997). "A Profile of women entrepreneurs and enterprises in Poland." Journal of Small Business Management 35(4): 76-82.

Zaobao Singapore (Chinese Newspaper). 21 August 2009. 13th Infocomm Commerce Conference. Singapore Press Holdings.

ABOUT THE AUTHOR

Dr Harold Siow Song Teng, PhD.

Dr Harold Siow Song Teng is Research Fellow & Administrative Manager at the Centre on Asia and Globalization (CAG) at the Lee Kuan Yew School of Public Policy, National University of Singapore. He was Visiting Scholar at the East Asian Institute, National University of Singapore from 2010-2011. Before embarking on an academic career, he has been an entrepreneur and a small business owner and has worked both in the private as well as public sectors.

He was formerly a Civil Servant in the Singaporean external trade promotion body International Enterprise Singapore, a statutory board under the Ministry of Trade and Industry and also served in the Ministry of Information, Communications and the Arts, Singapore. His research interests focus on ASEAN-China, Sino-Singapore, Singapore-Vietnam, Sino-Vietnam international political economy, economic and trade related issues.

He holds a PhD in Business and Management and Graduate Diploma in Management Research from the International Graduate School of Business, University of South Australia; a Master in Economics and Bachelor in Economics & Finance from the University of Sydney and Murdoch University, Australia respectively.

ENDNOTES

[1] Author's interview with Mr Ted Tan, Deputy CEO of International Enterprise Singapore on 12th February 2009.
[2] Ibid
[3]Ibid & Spring Singapore on 23rd Feb 2009 and from SME 21 Committee.
[4] For more details, see Ministry of Finance, Singapore www.mof.gov.sg
[5] International Enterprise (IE) Singapore is an agency under the Ministry of Trade and Industry spearheading the development of Singapore's external economy wing. Their mission is to promote the overseas growth of Singapore-based enterprises and international trade. With a global network in over 30 locations and their '3C' framework of assistance namely: Connections, Competency, Capital, they offer services to help enterprises export, develop business capabilities, find overseas partners and enter new markets. At the same time, they work to position Singapore as a base for foreign businesses to expand into the region in partnership with Singapore-based companies. Their vision is for Singapore to be a thriving business hub with globally competitive enterprises and leading international traders.
[6] Spring Singapore is the agency for enterprise development in Singapore. Its aims are to enhance the competitiveness of enterprises. Spring Singapore helps nurture a pro-business environment, facilitates the growth of industries and enhances innovation and enterprise capabilities of small and medium enterprises (SMEs) for better access to markets and business opportunities.
[7] "Key Government Assistance Programmes for SMEs" published by International Enterprise Singapore, Singapore Workforce Development Agency, Spring Singapore (2010). Additional information from the face-to-face interviews conducted with International Enterprises Singapore and Spring Singapore.
[8] Computed on a group basis where 20%-100% of the shares are owned by other companies; if a company owns 51%-100% of another company (subsidiary), the subsidiary's fixed assets and employees will also be added to the computation.
[9] HQ functions refer to activities such as banking and finance, marketing and business planning, procurement/ logistics, training and personnel management, investing planning/ coordination, research and development (R&D), technical support and manufacturing.
[10] Group is defined as the company and its directly owned subsidiaries and associate companies.
[11] Trade Credit Insurance is offered by Marsh Singapore Private Limited
[12] SEEDS Capital Private Limited a subsidiary company of Spring Singapore
[13] For more information, see 'Managerial Talent in SMEs' (2008)
[14] For more details, see 'Bosses go back to school to learn biz management' (2009)
[15] The Singapore Workforce Development Agency (WDA) seeks to enhance the employability and competitiveness of our workforce to meet the changing needs of Singapore's economy. Working with industry, unions, employers, economic

agencies, professional associations and training organizations, WDA's efforts are targeted at supporting industry growth by building a pipeline of workers through training and skills upgrading, and raising industry standards through enhancing manpower capabilities. For more details, see www.wda.gov.sg

[16] 'Spring Singapore Launches $30 million Incubator Development Programme' (2009).

[17] 'Trade Minister says Singapore Poised to Weather Downturn' (2009).

[18] Speech by Mr Lee Yi Shyan, Minister of State for Trade and Industry (2009).

[19] Data as of 16 Feb 2009.

[20] Speech by Mr Lee Yi Shyan, Minister of State for Trade and Industry (2009).

[21] 'Spring Builds Local Enterprises for the Future' (2009).

[22] 'Spring Builds Local Enterprise for the Future' (2009)

[23] The six EDCs are located within the offices of the Association of Small and medium-sized Enterprises (ASME); the Singapore Chinese Chamber of Commerce & Industry (SCCCI); the Singapore Indian Chamber of Commerce (SICCI); the Singapore Manufacturers' Federation (SMa); the Singapore Malay Chamber of Commerce & Industry (SMCCI); the Singapore Business Federation (SBF).

[24] 'Spring Builds Local Enterprise for the Future' (2009)

[25] 'Spring Builds Local Enterprise for the Future' (2009)

[26] For details see Atkinson, R. D., Andes, S.M. (2009).

[27] 'Singapore is the World's Easiest Place to do business' (2009).

[28] 'Singapore is 2nd Freest Economy' (2009).

[29] 'Doing Business? Singapore is Fourth Best' (2009).

[30] 'Singapore Taps Reserves for S$20.5 b Economic Stimulus Plan' (2009).

[31] 'SPUR-JOBS to provide up to S$400k in co-funding recruitment, training' (2009).

[32] 'Singapore Government Allocates S$600 million for Skills Upgrading' (2008).

[33] 'Singapore Government to Provide Extra S$2.3 billion in Loan Support to Businesses' (2008).

[34] 'Government Initiatives (SPUR & Jobs Credit Scheme)' (2009).

[35] 'Jobless? Be an SME Adviser' (2009).

[36] 'Government-backed Loans double in a Month' (2009).

[37] The members of the ESC include: 1) Mr Tharman Shanmugaratnam (Finance Minister); 2) Dr Ng Eng Han (Education Minister); 3) Mr Raymond Lim (Transport Minister); 4) Mr Gan Kim Yong (Manpower Minister); 5) Mrs Lim Hwee Hua (Minister in the Prime Minister's Office & 2nd Minister for Finance & Transport); 6) Rear Admiral Lui Tuck Yew (Acting Minister for Information, Communications & the Arts); 7) Ms S. Iswaran (Senior Minister of State for Trade & Industry, Education); 8) Ms Grace Fu (Senior Minister of State for National Development & Education); 9) Mr Heng Swee Keat (Managing Director, Monetary Authority of Singapore); 10) Mr Lim Swee Say (Secretary-General National Trade Union Congress & Minister in the Prime Minister's Office); 11) Mrs Josephine Teo (NTUC Assistant Secretary-General); 12) Mr Gautam Banerjee (Executive Chairman, PricewaterhouseCoopers Singapore); 13) Mr Tony Chew (Chairman, Singapore Business Federation); 14) Ms Deborah Henretta (Group

President, Procter & Gamble Asia); 15) Mr Lothar Hermann (ASEAN CEO, Siemens); 16) Mr Jason Jiang (CEO & Holding's Chairman, Focus Media); 17) Dr Jan-Anders Karlsson (CEO, S*Bio); 18) Mr James Koh (Deputy Chairman & MD, Koda); 19) Mr Lim Ming Yan (Capitaland China Holdings CEO); 20) Ms Shirlene Noordin (Phish Communications Director); 21) Mr Viswanathan Shankar (Standard Chartered Bank's Chairman for principal finance and private banking); 22) Dr Ricky Souw (Sanwa Group CEO & President of Singapore Precision Engineering and Tools Association); 23) Mr Tan Mok Koon (CSE Global Group MD); 24) Mr Wong Fong Fui (Boustead Singapore's Chairman and CEO); 25) Prof Bernard Yeung (Dean of NUS Business School).

[38] 'Diverse line-up for growth ideas' (2009).

[39] 'Rise of the new Entrepreneur' (2009).

[40] 'Beyond Stewardship: 50 Years of the MOF 1959-2009' (2009).

[41] For more details, see Inland Revenue Authority of Singapore (IRAS) www.iras.gov.sg

[42] For more details, see Accounting and Corporate Regulatory Authority of Singapore (ACRA) www.acra.gov.sg

[43] For more details, see "EnterpriseOne Portal" at www.business.gov.sg accessed on 23 July 2009

[44] 'Help for SMEs to Tap Internet for Growth' (2009).

[45] '13th Infocomm Commerce Conference' (2009).

[46] See www.insis.com

[47] For more information, see Asia Sentinel, 'Singapore's Temasek Stumbles Again' 16 November 2008 available online at www.asiasentinel.com accessed on 19 March 2010

[48] Spring Singapore is the enterprise development agency for growing innovative companies and fostering a competitive SME sector. They work with partners to help enterprises in financing, capabilities and management development, technology and innovation, and access to markets. As the national standards and accreditation body, SPRING also develops and promotes internationally-recognized standards and quality assurance to enhance competitiveness and facilitate trade.

[49] International Enterprise (IE) Singapore is the lead agency under the Ministry of Trade and Industry spearheading the development of Singapore's external economic wing. Their mission is to promote the overseas growth of Singapore-based enterprises and international trade. With a global network in over 30 locations and their '3C'framework of assistance – Connections, Competency, Capital, they offer services to help enterprises export, develop business capabilities, find overseas partners and enter new markets. At the same time, they work to position Singapore as a base for foreign businesses to expand into the region in partnership with Singapore-based companies. Their mission is for Singapore to be a thriving business hub with globally competitive enterprises and leading international traders. IE Singapore is also the official source of Singapore's trade statistics; it publishes statistics covering annual, cumulative, quarterly and monthly trade volumes and values of Singapore's imports, exports, re-exports and domestic

exports of all commodities in both HS SITC Codes and SITC (Standard International Trade Classification) codes.

[50] The Economic Development Board (EDB) is the organization responsible for the continued economic success of Singapore and the companies on its shores. Its mission is to make Singapore a compelling global hub for business and investment and create sustainable GDP growth for Singapore with good jobs and business opportunities for its people.

[51] For more see Garson (2009).

[52] Ibid